THE WESTERN FRONTIER LIBRARY

*A TRIP TO THE
YELLOWSTONE NATIONAL PARK*

A TRIP
to the
YELLOWSTONE
NATIONAL PARK

in July, August, and
September, 1875

⋖§ §⋗

by WILLIAM MERSON

GENERAL W. E. STRONG
III

With an introduction by
RICHARD A. BARTLETT

UNIVERSITY OF OKLAHOMA PRESS

NORMAN

Library of Congress Catalog Card Number: 68–15670

New edition copyright 1968 by the University of Oklahoma Press, Publishing Division of the University. Composed and printed at Norman, Oklahoma, U.S.A., by the University of Oklahoma Press. First printing of the new edition.

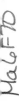

To

Hon. *Wm. W. Belknap*, Secretary of War

and

General *James W. Forsyth*, United States Army

To whom I am indebted for the most delightful trip of my life, and in memory of the fifty-three days passed in close companionship on railways and stage-coaches, on horseback and on the Missouri, this brief and imperfect journal of how we traveled and what we saw is respectfully inscribed by

WM. E. STRONG

Chicago, September 15, 1875

INTRODUCTION
≈§ §≈

By Richard A. Bartlett

ALL AGES and all societies have catered to their "Very Important Persons." Whatever the conditions, those favored few receive the very best that can be offered. They are idolized by the common folk, regaled with music, food, and verbose speeches, and made comfortable even if their servants shiver in the cold, eat leftovers, ride tired old mounts, and suffer from want of sleep. All of which may be very hard on the servants, a bore to the common people, and an obligation to the town fathers, but—let there be no doubt about it—it is great fun if you are a V.I.P.

This is the journal of a trip to the Yellowstone National Park taken in the summer of 1875 by a small party of V.I.P.'s from the East. They expected to receive the red carpet treatment as they traveled into the Wild West (for this was nearly a year before the Custer disaster on the Little Big Horn), and receive it they did. At Forts Saunders and Ellis, Buford and Berthold and Lincoln; at Camps Douglas and Baker and Lewis; at Salt Lake City and Ogden, Virginia City, Bozeman, Helena, Carroll and Bismarck, they were entertained in gala style. Silver cornet bands marched out to meet them. City fathers astride curried, beflagged, prancing horses, accompanied by any garishly dressed fire brigades available, led them to their quarters. The West put its best foot forward for these notables, and its hospitality left little to be desired.

When camp was established in Yellowstone, no less than twenty-four enlisted men, nine of whom were assigned as orderlies, chopped wood, started fires, prepared meals, pitched tents, polished boots, and cleaned guns for these prominent travelers.

Who were these V.I.P.'s? Initially there were four of them. Two entrained at Washington: they were General William Worth Belknap, Grant's secretary of war, and General Randolph Barnes Marcy, inspector general of the army. At Chicago they were joined by General James William Forsyth, who was serving on Sheridan's staff, and by General William Emerson Strong, the only non-career officer (other than Belknap) among them. Out west they would be joined by Lieutenant Gustavus C. Doane, General Nelson Bowman Sweitzer, and Colonel George L. Gillespie. These men, as part of their duties, would accompany the initial four and share the privileges.

The most notable member was, of course, General Belknap, a handsome, "pouchy-cheeked, beetle-browed, curly haired," bewhiskered man. Forty-six years old at the time, he was a graduate of Princeton and had been admitted to the bar in 1851. He went west to Iowa to grow up with the country, and by 1857 was sitting in the legislature as a Douglas Democrat. During the Civil War he had led the Fifteenth Iowa Infantry as a brigadier general. He commanded the Fourth Division of the Seventeenth Corps, of which the Fifteenth Iowa was a part. He was brevetted major general in March, 1865. Every promotion he had received was won on the battlefield.

After the war he became collector of internal revenue for

Iowa, but later was appointed secretary of war by Grant, the third and longest lasting (1869–76) of the five appointments to that office which Grant made.

There is no indication in Strong's Journal that Belknap was bothered by a guilty conscience or a brooding fear of exposure, unless his severe headaches can be attributed to a psychological origin; but less than six months after his September return to Washington, he was accused of malfeasance in office, impeached by a unanimous vote in the House of Representatives, and allowed to resign. Grant accepted his denial partly because, as a second lieutenant, Grant had served under Belknap's father, who had been a general. Although there is a slight justification for excusing the Secretary for all but incredible naïveté, the facts rather solidly point to his obvious and conscious guilt.[1]

The most warmly remembered person in the party, at least by historians of the Old West, was Randolph B. Marcy, inspector general of the army. Although sixty-three years of age in 1875, he was still youthful and vigorous. Marcy was an Academy man, who in 1851 had commanded General Belknap's military escort in a survey to locate military post sites in the Southwest. He had also explored the headwaters of the Red and Canadian rivers, had participated in 1857 in the so-called Mormon War, and had been chief of staff to his son-in-law, General George B. McClellan, in the Civil War. He was also a writer of some merit, compiling a semiofficial handbook entitled *The Prairie Traveler* in 1859, and later

[1] *Dictionary of American Biography*, II, 147–48; Allan Nevins, *Hamilton Fish: The Inner History of the Grant Administration* (New York, 1936), 804–10, quotation on p. 806.

writing *Thirty Years of Army Life on the Border* and *Border Reminiscences*. Described as being "tall, broad-shouldered, and soldierly in bearing," Marcy was the hunting expert of the group and was so addicted to trout fishing that he brought serious illness upon himself while in the Yellowstone.[2]

Next in the foursome was General James William Forsyth, another West Point graduate, forty years old and at midstream in a long army career. At war's end he was Sheridan's chief of staff, later his aide-de-camp, and finally secretary of the Division of the Missouri. Forsyth's career was marred by the stigma of the Sioux massacre at Wounded Knee, December 29, 1890, at which he was the commanding officer.[3] Strong declared him the champion storyteller of the party.

The fourth member and chronicler of the expedition was Brevet General William Emerson Strong. A lawyer and businessman of Chicago, related by marriage and retainers to the wealthy Ogden family, he was thirty-five years old on August 10, 1875 (which called for a celebration in the Park, complete with champagne, claret, and ginger ale). A native of New York State, he had grown up on a Wisconsin farm, had studied law at Racine, and had been admitted to the bar in 1861.

The Civil War changed the course of Strong's life. He raised a company of volunteers and led it as their captain at Bull Run. He was promoted to major with the Twelfth Wisconsin and saw service in Missouri, Kansas, and New Mexico; he was with the Army of the Tennessee when it took Vicks-

[2] *Dictionary of American Biography*, XII, 273–74. An excellent biography is W. Eugene Hollon, *Beyond the Cross Timbers: The Travels of Randolph B. Marcy*, 1812–1887 (Norman, 1955).

[3] Ezra J. Warner, *Generals in Blue: Lives of the Union Commanders* (Baton Rouge, 1964), 156–57.

burg, by which time he was lieutenant colonel. By 1864 he was inspector general of the Department of the Army of the Tennessee and later chief of staff to General Oliver O. Howard in the march through the Carolinas. He was promoted to colonel and on March 21, 1865, was brevetted major general of Volunteers. He ended his career as inspector general of the Freedmen's Bureau, from which office he resigned in September, 1866. For the remainder of his life he was in business, although he at least participated in Republican politics, being sergeant at arms at the National Convention in 1880. He died in Italy in April, 1891, at the age of fifty.[4]

Strong made lasting friendships with men in high places, and the mastic that held them together was the good life out of doors—hunting, fishing, and the companionship of campfire and wilderness trail. For fifty-three days he was with his associates on this "most delightful trip" of his life; again in 1878 he would be with a similar party, this time hunting turkeys along the Canadian River in Indian Territory (now Oklahoma) with Generals Sheridan, Whipple, and Crook.[5] In 1882 he would be in Yellowstone again with Sheridan, entering from the south after detraining at Green River. In his report of this trip, one of the officers said that the party named one of their camps "after our knightly and distin-

---

[4] New York *Times*, April 11, 1891, p. 4. During part of his Civil War Service, Strong was on the staff of General James McPherson. See Lt. Col. J. F. Gregory, "Report," in *Report of Lieut. General P. H. Sheridan . . . of His Expedition through the Big Horn Mountains* (Washington, 1882).

[5] General William E. Strong, *Canadian River Hunt* (Norman, 1960).

guished guest and sportsman, General William E. Strong."[6]
A vigorous leader of men, a good companion, a clear and
descriptive writer, and a sketchbook artist of some merit, it is
to General Strong that we owe this gem of a journal.

Out west the foursome would be joined from time to time
by many officers, but three of them were with the party in
Yellowstone Park and thus deserve special mention. Colonel
George L. Gillespie, Corps of Engineers, an Academy man
and a Medal of Honor recipient, had been on Sheridan's staff
during the war. He had already left for Fort Ellis, near Bozeman, Montana Territory, to make preparations for the trip
into the Park. General Nelson Bowman Sweitzer, another
Academy man, had seen frontier service with the First and
Second Dragoons in the 1850's, and had been McClellan's
aide-de-camp during part of the Civil War. Forty-six years
old in 1875, he was commanding officer at Fort Ellis.[7]

The third officer, and the guide into the Park, was Lieutenant Gustavus C. Doane, who was stationed at Fort Ellis with
the Second Cavalry. A graduate of the University of the
Pacific, a Civil War veteran, and an ambitious careerist, this
thirty-five-year-old officer had already been into the Park
several times. He was there with Washburn and Langford in
1870, and his report of that expedition had attracted Belknap's
attention.

Indeed, from 1871 on, the Secretary of War manifested a

[6] Lt. Col. J. F. Gregory, "Report," p. 11.

[7] George W. Cullum, *Biographical Register of the Officers and
Graduates of the U.S. Military Academy at West Point, New York*
(3d ed. rev., Boston, 1891), II, pp. 350, 571; West Point Alumni
Foundation, *Register of Graduates and Former Cadets of the United
States Military Academy, Civil War Centennial Edition* (1965), II,
241, 251.

keen interest in the Park. It may have been due to his influence that there was so much army activity there during his years in office. In the summer of 1871, Captain J. W. Barlow accompanied Ferdinand V. Hayden into the upper Yellowstone (Strong refers to Barlow's report, which he read on the way); in 1872, General John Gibbon explored the Park, followed in 1873 by Captain William A. Jones, and in 1875, along with the Secretary's own expedition, Captain William Ludlow of the Engineers led a reconnaissance from Carroll, Montana (on the Missouri River, about 166 miles east of Fort Benton) into the Park. In succeeding years Doane would return to the reservation, and many army men of distinction, including Generals Sherman and Sheridan, would camp there.[8]

As for the Belknap-Marcy-Forsyth-Strong expedition of 1875, there is no doubt that the Secretary was the instigator. His concern over the Park was but a reflection of the growing uneasiness among army men that "Wonder Land" was being destroyed and that its supervision by the Interior Department left much to be desired.

That army men should care about the Park may come as a surprise until it is remembered that the Civil War produced many officer-outdoorsmen who loved hunting and fishing. They were witnesses to the destruction of the buffalo and the threatened extinction of elk, deer, antelope, and bear, even in places as remote as Yellowstone. These men became ardent conservationists in order to preserve some areas, and some animals, for sportsmen.

It is significant that Strong, who alone caught more trout

[8] Hiram Martin Chittenden, *The Yellowstone National Park*, ed. by Richard A. Bartlett (Norman, 1964), 90–93.

than the entire party could possibly consume, and killed whole coveys of dusky grouse, and who might well have reflected upon his own gluttony, should have discussed the depletion of the game in the Park. The wholesale slaughter of the deer and elk for commercial purposes appalled him as it did all good Nimrods. He felt such wanton killing would soon exterminate the game and end the fun for the true sportsmen, who, under proper supervision, should be allowed to hunt in the Park for years to come.

Among army men there was also the feeling, never far beneath the surface, that rightfully the military should have the assignment of protecting and administering the Park. The Department of the Interior was an interloper, placed there by political chicanery or Congressional stupidity. Clearly, the army wanted control, and its maneuvers from the 1870's on finally achieved for it the policing assignment in 1886.

Thus, for Belknap the trip was more than a vacation. In his Annual Report for 1875 he expressed the wish of his department "to unite with the Secretary of the Interior in doing what is possible . . . for the opening and surveying of this region, so appropriately called 'Wonder Land.' " He then suggested that the Engineer Corps could build roads to the interior of the Park for "a modest sum." He added that the curiosities of the Park were being rapidly destroyed, and that, if authority were given, the army could "station one or two companies of troops in or near the park for the purpose of preventing spoliation. . . . Surely everything should be done that can be to protect all that is grand and beautiful in that remarkable region."[9]

[9] *Report of the Secretary of War for 1875* (Washington, 1876), I, 27–28.

And so the trip began. On Tuesday, July 15, the foursome left Chicago "at half-past ten o'clock." (Strong's habit of giving precise statistics for time and mileage and number of fish caught and grouse shot is characteristic of the times when, perhaps, men were not so busy as they are today, and made more of a fetish of precision statistics about such ordinary things.)

At Omaha the travelers were entertained by Generals Crook, Smith, Dodge, and other officers. Entrained again, the foursome played whist and told stories, but never were the hours too many before a community or an army post came into view. At Laramie the commanding officer of nearby Fort Saunders met them with the post band, which gave them a concert as they dined. General Forsyth's stories, apparently very humorous, were still holding out well.

Strong described the settlements, the wild life, and the scenery they saw along the Union Pacific. They visited Salt Lake City and Camp Douglas and feasted on ripe cherries and admired the orchards. Then they headed north through Ogden and Corinne to Franklin, where they climbed aboard a Concord coach for the long trip to Montana Territory. In order to make room for themselves, they pushed aside a would-be passenger named Philetus W. Norris. He took a very dim view of this act of rudeness, commenting upon their rosy out-look caused by a never ending supply of liquor.[10] Apparently, however, they were generous with it. Strong liked to sit up with the driver, but was quite shocked when he discovered

[10] Norris Papers, Henry E. Huntington Library. Norris was the second superintendent of the Yellowstone Park, but his appointment was not until 1877.

that his inebriated coachman had dozed off while the Concord was spinning along a narrow road cut in the mountainside.

On July 25, ten days out of Chicago, the party arrived at Virginia City, where they were called upon by a "large number of officials and prominent people of the town." Then they drove on to Bozeman in a comfortable Troy coach, and were met near there by the local silver cornet band, which escorted them into the flag-bedecked town where the Secretary received a seventeen-gun salute. A detachment of cavalry escorted the party on to Fort Ellis, where General Sweitzer met them.

In two ambulances, the most comfortable conveyances the frontier army possessed, the travelers set out for the Park. They were accompanied by General Sweitzer, Colonel Gillespie, and an escort, which went ahead to be on the lookout for Indians. At noon they reached Bottler's ranch, about halfway between Ellis and Mammoth Hot Springs (which Strong called Soda Mountain).

They camped at Soda Mountain, where Lieutenant Doane had just arrived with the pack train. With the addition of Assistant Surgeon Robert M. Whitefoot, their party was now complete; with twenty-four enlisted men and four noncommissioned officers, the entire party numbered thirty-five men.

At this camp the ambulances were left behind, and horses were furnished to the party along with mules to carry the equipment. The men visited the Grotto, Devil's Kitchen, and the Great Cave, none of which are subjects for inspection by tourists today. They then headed east-southeast toward Tower Falls, camping for the night along Black Tail Deer Creek, doing some hunting, and meeting a prominent early Yellowstone character, Jack Baronett. He owned a toll bridge across the Yellowstone, a few hundred yards south of the present bridge on the Northeast Entrance road. The next night they camped at Tower Falls.

On July 31 the party climbed Mount Washburn and then headed for the Grand Canyon, pausing en route to look at some sulphur springs. They missed the trail and became enmeshed in the jackstraw lodge-pole pine forest that caused many an explorer to curse the Yellowstone. By mid-afternoon, however, they had reached the great falls.

The next day Strong caught his first trout in the Yellowstone. He resorted to bait fishing only after an hour during which he had used every fly in his possession to no avail. His first trout weighed four pounds; by mid-afternoon he had caught thirty-five, none weighing under two and one-half pounds. General Marcy was so elated that he continued fishing even after falling into the river and getting soaked. He soon would regret his actions.

They camped at the Mud Volcano, which was a relatively new phenomenon in the 1870's that covered nearby trees with mud which soon would kill them. On August 2 they crossed over the mountains to the Lower Geyser Basin, and the next day worked southward to the Upper Basin. By now, however, General Marcy was quite ill, and for an extra day they remained in camp. They improvised a litter for him, suspended it between two gentle mules, and carried him back to the Mud Volcano. They then went on to the Yellowstone Lake, where they were amazed at the abundance of wild fowl.

After their return, they left Mud Volcano on August 8 for the long trek back to Fort Ellis. They followed approxi-

mately the same route they had taken previously. Jack Baronett, however, took Strong on a long day's hunt, ascending
the mountains west of Washburn and traveling north and
then east along the ridges. By evening they rejoined the main
party and camped close to Baronett's cabin near the junction
of the Lamar (then called the East Fork) and the Yellowstone. On August 10 they reached Soda Mountain, where
they celebrated Strong's birthday, and on the eleventh they
were back at Fort Ellis. All together they had spent thirteen
days in the Park.

They left Fort Ellis on August 14 planning to return home
via the Missouri River. First they went to Helena, which was
out of the way. Strong does not specify why they took this
route, but it was probably due to Indian depredations along
the more direct road from Ellis to Camp Baker. It was safer
to go up to Helena and then along the so-called Carroll road.
This led northeast to that small community, located on the
Missouri near the mouth of the Musselshell, not the Judith,
as Strong incorrectly states.[11] It was on this part of the trip
that Strong experienced the thrills of a buffalo hunt which
left him so sore that for several days thereafter he declined to
go hunting.

They descended the Missouri by steamboat, stopping at
Forts Peck, Buford, and Berthold on the way to Bismarck.
There they transferred to the Northern Pacific railroad. They
took a diversionary trip down to Fort Lincoln, however, to

[11] William Ludlow, *Report of a Reconnaissance from Carroll,
Montana Territory, on the Upper Missouri, to the Yellowstone Park,
And Return, Made in the Summer of 1875* (Washington, 1876),
12–16.

visit General Custer and his lady, and Strong's descriptions shed much light on the personality of that flamboyant officer.

The visit was also to give rise to a rumored snub administered to Belknap by Custer. Military courtesy prescribed that the commanding officer should meet the Secretary at the reservation boundary, but, so the report went, Custer met Belknap in his office.[12] He verified this in testimony before an investigating committee, apparently trying thereby to dissociate himself from any connections with the discredited Belknap. ". . . I knew of his coming and gave him such attention as his official position required," Custer said; "a salute was fired, but my knowledge of his transactions and my opinion of them was such that I did not meet him at the edge of the reservation, as was customary. I stayed at my door and waited till he came, and transacted what business I had to transact with him, and he went away."[13]

Belknap was shocked at this statement, which did not agree with his own memory of the events, and he wrote to General Forsyth for his support in refuting Custer's testimony. Forsyth replied in a letter to Belknap which was published by the *Army and Navy Journal* for April 22, 1876. The understanding at the time, Forsyth explained, had been that Custer was ill,

[12] Jay Monaghan, *Custer: The Life of General George Armstrong Custer* (Boston, 1959), 261; Frederic F. Van de Water, *Glory Hunter: A Life of General Custer* (Indianapolis, 1934), 265; Edgar I. Stewart, *Custer's Luck* (Norman, 1955), 127.

[13] Earl K. Brigham, "Custer's Meeting with Secretary of War Belknap at Fort Abraham Lincoln," *North Dakota History*, Vol. XIX, No. 2 (April, 1952), pp. 129–30. The testimony was before the so-called Clymer Committee, whose report was entitled "Sale of Post Traderships," 44 Cong., 1 sess., *House Report No. 799* (Washington, 1876), quotation on page 157.

that he had risen from a sick bed, donned his uniform, and met the Secretary at the sidewalk in front of his house. In spite of his illness he spared nothing to give the Secretary and his party a pleasant stay. The letter, which portrays essentially the same tone about the visit as the Strong description, completely discredits Custer's testimony, and does his name no good.[14]

By September 4 the Northern Pacific had carried the party to Fargo, and St. Paul was reached by the fifth. There General Terry greeted them and gave them a hearty breakfast; on September 6 they arrived back in Chicago.

To General William Emerson Strong it had been a wonderful trip, the kind that mellows into nostalgia with the passing of time. How many parties of fishermen catch over three thousand trout? He had his journal privately printed, replete with photographs of the members and a few sketches of events along the way. Everyone seemed to be happy with it except the critical editor of the Bozeman *Avant-Courier*, who resented Strong's reference to that Montana community as a "village," and added, "The General don't mention the champagne we paid for, which makes us hope it soured upon his stomach."[15] In 1965 a copy of the Journal sold at auction for $180.

One proud possesser was Mr. Fred Schonwald, a book collector from Oklahoma City, who died in December, 1966. He was delighted with the book's charm, and it was characteristic of his generous nature to want to share his find with others. He had planned to write the introduction, and his

[14] Brigham, *loc. cit.* The Forsyth letter is quoted extensively in this article.

[15] Bozeman *Avant-Courier*, February 15, 1877, p. 3.

copy of the journal is the one used for this edition. To Mr. Schonwald this reprint of the Strong journal is respectfully dedicated.

A few mundane matters demand clarification or correction. I have used the highest brevetted ranks for the army men. Notations within brackets indicate corrections. Minor punctuation changes also have been made, without notice, when the original punctuation might be confusing to the reader. Thanks are extended to the Henry E. Huntington Library for examination of the Norris papers and to that library and the American Philosophical Society for the financial aid that made possible my research there. Photographs of the illustrations were provided through the courtesy of the DeGolyer Foundation Library.

Finally, search as I did, inquire as I did from worldly-wise men, I failed to discover the "pithy" reply of the plump young German lady to the little barking dog, as related by General Forsyth on page 22. To anyone who can supply the missing line to this story, I hereby bestow the accolade, Researcher of the Year.

CONTENTS

ILLUSTRATIONS
❦

A TRIP TO THE
YELLOWSTONE NATIONAL PARK

A TRIP TO THE YELLOWSTONE NATIONAL PARK

ON THE 5TH OF JULY, 1875, I received an urgent invitation from the Secretary of War and General James W. Forsyth, U.S. Army, to join them in a trip to the National Park in Wyoming Territory, which I gladly accepted, believing it to be "the chance of a lifetime." I worked day and night for ten days to arrange my business satisfactorily, and on the evening of July 14th was fully prepared for a month's absence from Chicago.

As the country we were to travel over was almost wholly new to me, and as very little has been written of the wonders and beauties of the great Yellowstone Park, I resolved, for my own satisfaction, to keep a journal of the trip, of which the following is a copy:

July 15.—Left Chicago this morning at half-past ten o'clock, on Chicago and Northwestern Railroad. The party consists of General W.W. Belknap, Secretary of War; General Randolph B. Marcy, Inspector General, U.S.A.; General James W. Forsyth, U.S.A.; and William E. Strong, of Chicago.

Colonel George L. Gillespie, U.S. Corps of Engineers, has gone on in advance of us to Fort Ellis, Montana, to perfect the arrangements for our trip from that point to the Park, such as organizing and equipping the pack-train, selecting saddle-horses for the party, and getting together the necessary

3

supplies and camp equipage for a trip such as we have in view. All the party are well provided with guns and fly-rods and tackle. Mrs. Strong and little Ogden and General Sheridan were at the depot to see us off, and as the train pulled out wished us a pleasant journey, a good time, and an early and safe return.

The weather was cool and comfortable throughout the day, and we all enjoyed to the fullest extent the ride over the magnificent prairies of Illinois and Iowa.

I have spent most of the day in reading Captain Barlow's report of his exploration of the Yellowstone Park in July and August, 1871, and in studying his map of the country lying between Fort Ellis and Yellowstone Lake. I had before this no conception of the marvelous things to be seen in the country we are traveling to. Find General Marcy a most agreeable traveling companion, and the stories he is able to relate to frontier life and campaigning, and the killing of big game in the mountains and plains of the West, are of intense interest to me. The General is the keenest sportsman and one of the most noted hunters in the Army. I like him very much, and I shall enjoy hunting and fishing with him, I know. The Secretary is a good storyteller, and has some excellent ones on himself, which he narrates as readily as though the jokes were on some one else. General Forsyth, however, is the champion story-teller of the party. His stock is inexhaustible, and in all my life I have never met with his equal. I have traveled with him before, and know very well his capabilities in this direction. Everything he sees or hears reminds him of a story, and his peculiar style is original and unapproachable; never tells a story twice alike, but touches it up and improves it each time—

4

General W. W. Belknap
Secretary of War

indeed, he makes a good story out of the most trivial incident.

With Forsyth, Belknap, and Marcy in the party I do not see how time can hang very heavily on our hands. I have been wondering to myself whether their stock of stories will last to Fort Ellis.

July 16.—We passed a very comfortable night, and reached Council Bluffs, at 9:30 A.M., where General Granville M. Dodge met us. The Secretary, having some business of importance to attend to here, stopped over for the day with General Dodge, but is to join us at the hotel in Omaha this evening.

After an hour or more spent in transferring baggage (which unnecessary proceeding is enough to exhaust the patience of Job), we crossed the Missouri River, and at 11 A.M. were in our rooms at the Grand Hotel in Omaha. General Crook and some of his Staff met us at the depot and accompanied us to the hotel. We are to dine with him this evening.

The arrangement now is to leave Omaha to-morrow morning for the West. General Crook and General William S. Smith, of Chicago, are to accompany our party as far as Cheyenne, at which point they leave us, en route for the Black Hills.

The weather has been intensely hot to-day, and I do not know when I have suffered so much. Called upon General and Mrs. Crook this evening, and passed an hour or more very pleasantly. Met General and Mrs. Smith, and returned to the hotel early.

July 17.—Left Omaha at 11:30 A.M. General Dodge, General Davis, and number of officers from the barracks were at the depot to see us off. Rained very hard last night, but the weather to-day is cool and delightful—a pleasant change from yesterday. The day's journey along the Platte Valley has been rather dull and monotonous, through a vast, fertile plain as far west as Columbus, and with a strong, rich soil, producing the finest of wheat, corn, oats, and vegetables, and this section is quite densely populated. We passed during the night the memorable and once celebrated stations of Forts Kearney and McPherson.

Along this great line of railway in 1867 and 1868 sprung up in a day, as it were, embryo "cities," which grew and flourished until the iron rails were laid beyond them, when they were abandoned in a night for a location further to the front, which promised a richer harvest to the speculator and gambler.

These stations along the Union Pacific Railroad were all famous in their day—1867 and 1868—but are now almost entirely forgotten. The ruins of deserted adobe houses and the neglected graves of their occupants, who went down, revolver in hand and with their boots and spurs on, are the only reminders now of the existence of these once famous towns. General Marcy informed us that upon one of the headboards which a few years since marked the graves of the departed pioneers of Green River was the following touching epitaph:

"Here rests the body of Bob. Jenkins. He was one of the right sort, but was shot in the back by a cowardly s—— of a b—— while goin' his bottom dollar on a squar' game of 'draw.' "

The day has passed pleasantly with us. Some good stories have been told by the Secretary and General Forsyth, among the best of which was the Secretary's story of the drunken man who declared that "it did him high honor to be in the presence of the great Belk-Knap of the Navy."

After reading Chicago papers of the 16th, the Secretary, General Marcy, General Crook, and myself played whist till the train reached Grand Island. A package of mosquito medicine, from Mr. George Walker, of Chicago, came to hand this morning, which was gratifying to us all, as we learn that mosquitos and flies are very numerous in the Yellowstone country.

July 18.—Last night was so cool that we all slept soundly, and awoke this morning much refreshed. The scenery as far west as Cheyenne was very much like that passed over yesterday, but our ride from Cheyenne to Laramie was more interesting, having distant views of Long's and Pike's Peaks and the Snowy Range.

After passing the border of Wyoming a new country spread out before and around us. The Plains continue everywhere, but are bounded on the south by visible foot-hills and outlying spurs of the Rocky Mountains.

Soon after leaving Cheyenne the scenery becomes bolder and more picturesque, and as we ascend the long, sharp grade from Cheyenne to Sherman we pass great mounds, hills, buttes, boulders, and rocks of the most singular formation.

At Sherman we cross the "backbone of the continent," eight thousand, two hundred and thirty-five feet above the level of the sea, and the highest railway station in America. So gradual is the ascent that one can hardly realize that such a great altitude has been attained. The descent from Sherman to the Laramie Plains is most charming, and from the rear platform of our car, the last in the train, we enjoyed the delightful sensation of "coasting," or "sliding down hill."

Arrived at Laramie at 6:30, where Colonel Bracket, commanding at Fort Saunders, with all the officers at the post, met us with the fine band of the Second Cavalry, and as soon as the train stopped the Drum Major came into our car and distributed to the party the following musical programme, which the band executed in fine style while we were eating supper:

COMPLIMENTS
of the
OFFICERS OF FORT SAUNDERS, WYOMING TERRITORY,
to
THE HON. SECRETARY OF WAR AND PARTY.

PROGRAMME.

1. Overture _____"Light Cavalry," _____Tuppe.
2. Polka _____"Luna." _____Peplow.
3. Grand Selection _"Bohemian Girl." _____Balfe.
4. Concert Waltz __"Immortellen." _____Gungl.
5. Potpourri _____"Popular Airs." _____J. H. B. Sullivan.

W. P. CLARK,
Adjutant 2d Cavalry.

After leaving Laramie and until it was quite dark, antelope in considerable numbers were seen on both sides of the railroad track, some of them within easy rifle-shot. Indeed, bands of eight or ten upon several occasions stood within a hundred yards of the railroad, quietly gazing at us as we went whirling by. We also saw a large gray wolf running side by side in apparent harmony with an antelope, and not to exceed four hundred yards from us. Occasionally they would both stop for an instant, look at the train, and then trot off quietly together, until they disappeared over a bluff.

8

General Crook, General Smith, wife and son, left our party at Cheyenne, en route for the Black Hills.

Weather still continued so cool that an overcoat was comfortable, and as there was no dust we have enjoyed the day immensely.

Forsyth's stock of stories still holds out, and I have laughed till I am exhausted. The Secretary has also given us some good ones. The best of all, I think, was his graphic description of the trials and tribulations of the President and Cabinet at the Centennial Celebration at Boston, Concord, and Lexington.

Salt Lake City.

July 19.—Last night was the coldest since leaving Chicago, and all of us required extra blankets, yet I never slept sounder in my life. We were up at an early hour for a good breakfast at Green River. Our appetites are getting wonderfully sharp.

At Green River we saw an immense wild-cat in a cage, which we learned had been caught in that vicinity, and I counted the heads and antlers of fifty-five black-tail deer, besides a number of elk and antelope heads, suspended on the fence near the entrance to the hotel. Game is said to be very abundant in this vicinity. Met Major Powell here.

The country west of Green River as far as Evanston is certainly the most worthless and God-forsaken I have ever seen—a barren and unproductive waste; vast plains of alkali and sage-brush, bordered by bluffs and buttes of picturesque form, many of them of indescribable beauty—a most welcome relief to the monotonous outlook during the hundreds of miles of level desert east of Green River. During the forenoon the

Wasatch range of mountains, the sides and peaks white with snow, has been in sight to the south of us, from sixty to eighty miles away, running nearly parallel to the railway track. Just after leaving Green River station we saw to the north, skirting the horizon, the Wind River range, and to the southeast the Uintah Mountains.

Throughout all this region west from Green River and along the line of the Union Pacific Railway, until we approach Evanston, great black buttes rise up on every side, hundreds of feet in height. An Eastern journalist, a traveler over this region in the early days of the Pacific Railway, has written a description of the varied shapes and fantastic forms which everywhere meet the eye. "All about one," he says, "lie long, wide troughs, as of departed rivers; long, level embankments, as of railroad tracks or endless fortifications; huge, quaint hills, suddenly rising from the plain, bearing fantastic shapes; great, square mounds of rock and earth; half-formed, half-broken pyramids, it would seem as if a generation of giants had built and buried here, and left their work to awe and humble a puny succession."

We dined at Evanston, on Bear River, seventy-eight miles from Ogden—the cleanest and most attractive eating-house we have yet seen. The proprietor of the hotel showed us a dozen or more large trout, weighing from five to seven pounds, which were caught in Bear Lake, forty miles distant. They call them lake trout, and we were told they would rise quickly to a fly.

Our ride from Evanston was lovely beyond description, and increased in grandeur and beauty as we approached Ogden, at which place we arrived at 6:30 P.M. It would take pages to describe with any satisfaction all that is seen from the railway car during the fifty miles just east from Ogden. I can only mention briefly the points of greatest interest. The great tunnel, eight hundred feet in length, near Wasatch Station; the lovely valley before the entrance to Echo Cañon, with the waters of the Weber River flowing smoothly and gently throughout it; while further on, with a current swift and strong, they dash over a rocky bed, forming cascades and rapids of wonderful beauty. Now we are opposite Castle Rock, at the head of Echo Cañon, where it has stood for centuries like a sentinel at his post, guarding the grand and majestic portal. And now we are spinning through the cañon itself, a narrow gorge between rocky and precipitous walls, rising hundreds of feet above the railroad track.

This tortuous cañon is hemmed in so closely by lofty, rugged cliffs that the sunlight is forever shut out. Every revolution of the engine's wheels, every stroke of the piston, shows the traveler something wild, new, and beautiful. We dash through this crooked gorge at lightning speed, and, before we know it, are rushing along a broad, quiet valley, where everything is bright, green, and fresh, past Echo City, and approach the grandest, wildest gorge of all, "Weber Cañon," the gigantic escarpments of which are higher, steeper, darker, and more picturesque than any I have ever beheld. Its sides are carved into fantastic shapes. Great rugged spurs shoot out and hang over the track, while beneath it the Weber River dashes, foams, and leaps like a huge mountain cataract over its stony bed, clinging closely to the railroad. The rush of the train and shrill whistle of the locomotive as it twists in and out, and swings around the sharp curves in the road, make one's blood fairly tingle with excitement and pleasure. The old stage-road follows the river and railroad through Echo Cañon, which the Mormons fortified to resist the advance of our troops in 1857. This we crossed and recrossed innumerable times, passing the famous "Thousand-mile tree," the "Devil's Gate," the "Devil's Slide," and Uintah Station, and shortly afterwards the train pulled up at Ogden.

We left Ogden at 7:30 P.M., reached Salt Lake City at 9 o'clock, and took lodgings at the Walker House, where I am sure we shall be comfortable.

July 20.—Breakfasted at 9 o'clock, and at 11 we accompanied General Belknap to Camp Douglas, where a salute was fired in honor of the Secretary of War, and we spent a couple of hours very agreeably. The Secretary and General Marcy were shown everything at the post, and the party was most hospitably entertained by Mrs. General John E. Smith and the officers of the Fourteenth Infantry, after which we returned to the hotel in time for lunch, when we rode about the city, visiting different places of interest, and spent some time in the Tabernacle, where great preparations were in progress for the annual celebration of the arrival in this Territory of Brigham Young and his flock. The church was being decorated by the Mormon women and young girls, and we watched their proceedings for some little time with considerable interest. After leaving the Tabernacle drove to the Sulphur Springs, and all indulged in a bath. Upon our return to the city we called upon Mrs. Jennings and her two daughters (Mormons), who received and entertained us most cordially and pleasantly. The youngest daughter was a bright, pretty girl, and conversed with ease and elegance. We were invited into the garden, where we feasted for some time on the most luscious cherries I ever saw. The house was quite handsomely furnished, and the grounds very attractive. Mr. Jennings is one of the Mormon leaders, and very wealthy, as we were informed.

Salt Lake City covers an area of about nine square miles, and is most beautifully laid out, with wide streets, having irrigating ditches on both sides, which are constantly filled with pure cold water from the mountains. The water is thus carried through every block. Shade trees also surround each block, and every house has an orchard of choice fruit. Indeed, I doubt if a city can be found anywhere as thoroughly policed, or with such fine orchards, magnificent shade trees, and such fresh, pure air as Salt Lake City. I certainly think the Mormons are a remarkable people, and are truly entitled to great credit for the wonderful work they have accomplished in this desert. It verily "blossoms like the rose," but it has taken years of toil and labor to cultivate and develop this valley of sagebrush and make it what we see it to-day. The farms we passed yesterday evening, between here and Ogden, are splendid, and I doubt if better wheat, oats, and barley can be grown anywhere.

We have been invited to go to the mines to-morrow, and also to the Lake and take an excursion in the steamer, but the Secretary, for want of time, has declined all invitations of this character, and wishes to push on to Fort Ellis as soon as possible.

The Fourteenth Infantry band serenaded the Secretary

this evening, playing for two hours or more in front of the hotel; after which the Secretary of War received the officers from Camp Douglas, with their wives.

July 21.—A number of leading Mormons paid their respects to the Secretary this morning at the hotel, among them a son of Brigham Young, who recently graduated, third in his class, at West Point, and has been assigned to the Corps of Engineers. He seems a bright, manly young fellow, and the Secretary says he was well thought of at the Military Academy.

We left Salt Lake at 3:30 P.M., accompanied as far as Ogden by several prominent Mormons, among whom were Mayor Wells, of Salt Lake City, late Lieutenant General of the Nauvoo Legion; Mr. Cannon, Delegate to Congress from this Territory; and Bishop Sharp, President of the Utah Northern Railroad, who was very kind to us.

We took supper at Ogden and left immediately afterwards for Franklin, upon the narrow-gauge road which skirts the northeastern shore of Salt Lake, while to the right of the road lays a continuous line of rugged bluffs and many fine farms, with neat, snug houses and barns, lying between the railway and foot-hills.

As we neared Corinne the country seemed much poorer, particularly to the west of us, where nothing could be seen but sagebrush, alkali, ant-hills, and sand. Soon after dark, however, we entered the famous "Cache Valley," which is said to be the richest and most prosperous section of Utah. Reached Franklin at 11 o'clock, and were met at the depot by Mr. Hatch, a Mormon of some prominence here. Bishop

Sharp telegraphed him from Ogden to meet our party and take care of us. He did his best, but accommodations are poor enough here, yet we made the best of it for one night. We have a long journey before us, and I fancy we will get tired of it before we reach Fort Ellis.

July 22.—We were up early, but as breakfast was a trifle late it was half-past five when we got into the coach and drove to the depot for our baggage. Our vehicle, which is to be our home for five days, is worthy of brief description. It is a great, swinging stage, known in this country as a Concord wagon, with immense thorough-braces, and as easy as a cradle on wheels, when well filled with passengers, and properly loaded and balanced.

At 6 o'clock we were ready for the start. The coach had pulled up at the village, and stopped near a whiskey-shop for the regular driver to take the reins. This dignitary, who soon appeared, was a slim-built man of five-and-thirty, and so very drunk that I could hardly believe we were to be conducted over our first run by a person in his condition. He had most remarkable control over his legs and hands, however, for he managed to reach the coach and climb to his seat without aid from any one. The Secretary, Generals Marcy and Forsyth were inside. I had chosen an outside seat, as I wanted to get a good view of the country. "Are you all ready?" says the driver. "All ready," was the response. Then gathering the reins carefully in his left hand and swinging his whip with the right, the lash cutting sharply across the flanks of the leaders, "Lee Goddard" (that was his name) exclaimed, "Git out of here, you pirates," and the next instant we were off, lead, swing, and wheel horses on the keen jump. Again and again the whip was applied, and thus we departed from Franklin at the rate of sixteen miles an hour.

The morning was superb, the whole landscape bright with the sunshine, just spreading out over valley and hill. The dew on the grass glittered and sparkled in the sunlight like precious gems. How fresh and pure the atmosphere! How exhilarating and exciting the furious, dashing pace at which we were whirled over the prairie!

For the first twelve miles the land was gently undulating, with a grand sweep of regular elevations and depressions as far as we could see. The intense pleasure to me of this first morning's ride in the great, swaying Concord wagon is indescribable. We were fairly afloat on the great plains of Idaho; free from all care and responsibility; no business letters to answer; no telegrams to head us off. We struck quite a long stretch of heavy road a few miles from Franklin, where even our tipsy Jehu was forced to walk his horses; and we reached the first station on Bear River, twelve miles out, in an hour and ten minutes. We jumped out and "stretched our legs," while a fresh relay of six handsome bays were hitched to the coach, and in five minutes were bowling along again, at the same killing pace. Goddard's run is to Port Neuf Cañon, sixty miles, and he changes five times, an average of twelve miles for each relay. From Bear River to Port Neuf Cañon the road was fearfully dusty, so that we were enveloped in great clouds hour after hour, and it seemed sometimes as though we would surely suffocate. For miles and miles the lead horses were entirely hidden, and very frequently all of the horses were lost to view; still Goddard cracked his whip, and made every horse do his best.

Lee Goddard is a character who was not inclined to be social early in the day, but later, as we became better acquainted, he talked freely and gave me his history. His life has been passed in California, New Mexico, and in the Territories, and his adventures would fill a book. Has been a stage-driver from early boyhood, and is very proud of his skill with the reins; but, unfortunately, his habits are very bad, and every few months the stage company discharges him, but always takes him back when he straightens up. He is the best driver on the line, and is spoken of everywhere as the most skillful reinsman in this country. He looked longingly at a demijohn under our feet, and finally mustered courage to say that if he had one good, square drink he was sure he could get us through to Port Neuf in time; but as the entire contents of the small flask we carried, exclusively for medicinal purposes, would not probably have come up to his estimate of a square drink, I declined the proposition. Later, and while we were making some sharp curves, where the narrow road was cut out from the mountain's side, with frightful precipices below us, I turned, and, to my astonishment, saw the driver nodding, and the reins hanging loosely in his hands. The situation was by no means pleasant. The horses were going rapidly, with a drunken driver fast asleep, and only a foot between the outer wheels and the brink of a precipice two hundred feet high, where, if a horse slipped and went down, or a wheel came off, there was no hope for us. In view of this, I grasped the reins, and at the same time shook the fellow gently until he awoke, when he very cooly asked, "Wha-ze matter?" and when I told him he had been sleeping, he laughed, saying, "Don't be skeert, ole fellar; them hosses, they knows the road, sure's yer born'd. Never upset a stage in my life. G'lang there," and at the same time he applied the whip to the swing horses, sending us along faster than ever.

At 5 o'clock we reached Port Neuf, covered with dust, and stopped for supper. This station is owned by Captain Harkness, of the Fifteenth Illinois Infantry, who came to Idaho in 1865, just after the war, and is making money here by raising stock. The place was clean and attractive, and we were in no hurry to leave. Goddard, I am happy to learn, goes no further, as I would not care to trust him for our night drive.

Left Port Neuf Station at 6:30 and drove hard all night. Our new driver is a sober, intelligent man, and we feel pretty safe with the reins in his hands. I rode outside till midnight and enjoyed every moment, although, at times, the road was exceedingly dusty, following the Port Neuf River and Cañon for twenty miles; and I have rarely had a lovelier ride. The river rushed along below us, and the scenery, viewed by moonlight, was of the wildest and most interesting description.

July 23.—Reached Corbet's Station, on Snake River, at 5 o'clock this morning, having accomplished one hundred and twenty miles of our journey, which the dust and heat have rendered exceedingly uncomfortable and fatiguing. The Secretary and General Marcy stood the ride remarkably well, however. After breakfasting at Corbet's we were on the road again at 6:30. Crossed Snake River on "Eagle Rock Bridge" at 11 o'clock, and about 4 in the afternoon arrived at "Sand Holes," where we had supper, having made sixty miles during the day. From Corbet's our driver rushed us through at the same rapid pace, and we made during the day eighteen miles, over a very rough road, in an hour and fifty minutes; sixteen miles in an hour and thirty minutes, and twelve miles in one hour.

Leaving the Sand Holes at 5 P.M., we arrived at Pleasant Valley at 2 this morning. About 11 o'clock we commenced the ascent of the Rocky Mountains, when it turned so cold that I was forced to go inside the coach, and as the stage drew up at Pleasant Valley Station we were all pretty thoroughly used up, having been riding continuously day and night for two hundred and twenty-six miles. From Corbet's to Sand Holes is a vast, unbroken plain, utterly worthless, except for grazing.

July 24.—We slept soundly last night, and awoke greatly refreshed. Breakfasted at 7:30, and were en route again at quarter after eight. The morning was bright, clear, and beautiful, with a fresh breeze blowing from the north. Our road soon led us to the summit of the Rocky Mountains, fourteen thousand feet above the sea, where the line dividing Montana and Idaho crosses our track, from whence we had a magnificent view of lofty mountain ranges, stretching away as far as the eye could reach on every side, presenting a surpassingly lovely coup d'oeil; and the little valley at our feet was a small rivulet that one could step over, while further on, and within sight, the stream divided, one branch bearing off to the south towards the Pacific Ocean, the other branch leading to the north and flowing into the Atlantic. The southern branch of this brook is an affluent of Snake River, one of the main tributaries of the Columbia; the other branch, one of the very head tributaries of the Missouri, after twisting and winding at the base of the mountains and buttes for a few miles, forms what is known as the "Red Rock River"; and fifty miles further on it is known as the Beaver Head River, which with the "Big Hole," or "Wisdom River," constitutes the Jefferson Fork, one of the principal tributaries of the great Missouri.

The Secretary took occasion to remark here that there was some point (he was not altogether positive where) on the road to Ellis which General Sheridan had spoken of as an appropriate place to drink to his health, and had especially requested him not to forget it. The decision was unanimous that this must be the identical spot referred to. Accordingly General Forsyth quickly opened a bottle of champagne, and we drank "Long life, health, happiness, and prosperity to General Sheridan and his bride."

Ten miles further on, after reaching the summit, the magnificent "Red Rock" Valley lay spread out like a picture before us. This valley lies hemmed in by mountains of great altitude, and is from one-and-a-half to two-and-a-half miles in width. The stream (Red Rock) winds along on the easterly side, and stretches away directly to the north. Its waters, sparkling in the early morning sunlight, seemed to us, from the great height at which looked upon it, like a thread of burnished gold, and we lingered here for some time, enjoying to the utmost this lovely valley and the stream which threaded it. The descent from this point was so difficult that we were obliged to walk, and the driver had his hands full in engineering the coach and horses safely down the fearfully precipitous mountain road.

Our course followed the "Red Rock" Valley and stream

for thirty-five miles, and I never saw a harder, smoother road. We fairly flew down this valley. The relays were capital, and they were made to do their best. One six-horse team of blooded bays made fourteen miles within the hour by the watch, enabling us to reach "Lovell's Station" at 7 o'clock, having traveled since morning seventy miles. Twelve miles south of Lovell's we struck the "Beaver Head River" and entered "Ryan's Cañon," where the road was extremely rough, but the wild and beautiful scenery here surpassed anything we have yet seen. The stage-road for several miles in this cañon has been cut from the sides of the mountain, and is barely wide enough for the coach, leaving no room for another vehicle to pass.

Bold mountains rise up hundreds of feet on either side of us, and the Beaver Head, flowing with dashing current at the bottom of a dizzy chasm far below our stage-route, rushes along over big bowlders and rocky ledges, forming a succession of rapids and cataracts of great variety and beauty. Half-way through this cañon the gorge narrows; the mountains are higher, more precipitous, and the angles sharper; and the chasm below us, through which the river holds its course, is deeper, darker, and more impressive. Nevertheless, through this wild gorge, and over this narrow, dangerous road, we passed at the break-neck pace of eight miles an hour.

The day's journey has been delightful—no dust, and the air fresh and bracing. We breakfasted at Pleasant Valley on elk meat and brook trout. We have made now two hundred and ninety-six miles of our stage-journey to Ellis, and expect to be at Virginia City to-morrow.

Virginia City.

July 25.—Reached Virginia City at 4:30 P.M., having traveled seventy miles. Our road followed the Beaver Head for thirty-five miles, through a fine grazing country, where we saw plenty of ranches with large herds of cattle and horses.

Dined at Gafney's twenty-eight miles from Virginia City. Soon after leaving Gafney's we struck the "Stinking Water Valley," and passed through the village of "Sheridan."

The last seven or eight miles of our day's journey was rough, and we were very glad when the comfortable hotel was reached. The day being Sunday we have tried to observe it to some extent, and the party has been unusually quiet. Some interesting camp-meeting incidents were narrated, however, by General Marcy, one of which provoked a smile all around. The circumstance occurred in the mountain regions of Pennsylvania with a young lady of German extraction, the development of whose vigorous physique had never been cramped by corsets or other modern appliances, and who, upon one occasion at a camp meeting, participated most zealously, but somewhat vehemently, in the exciting scenes of a revival, by throwing her feet and arms around in such a violent manner, while singing and shouting at the highest pitch of her voice, as to attract the attention of a small dog, who in his fright ran around her, barking and snapping at her feet furiously. Her response to these demonstrations constitutes the pith of the story, which is left for the reader to conjecture.

Virginia City, which has now a population of about seven or eight hundred, and from three hundred and fifty to four hundred voters, is situated in a mountain gorge known as "Alder Gulch," and has but one principal street.

Alder Gulch heads eight miles to the south of the city, at what is called the "Summit," and the "placer mining" is carried on all the way from the Summit to a point six miles below the city.

Mining operations were begun here in 1863, and from twenty-five to thirty millions of gold have been taken from Alder Gulch. During the height of the mining excitement in 1864, the population here exceeded twelve thousand, while at present there are not to exceed three hundred miners at work here. Something like five hundred thousand dollars in gold were taken out during 1874, and probably about the same amount will be found this year. From all I can learn, however, Virginia City has seen its best and most prosperous days, as it has been steadily losing ground for two or three years past. Most of the miners are Chinamen, who are working over the old ground.

By a vote of the people, at last fall's election, the Capital was moved to Helena, and General B. F. Potts, the Governor of the Territory, removed his headquarters to that place some two months since. We hear he is to meet us to-morrow afternoon at Bozeman, seventy-eight miles from this place and three miles from Ellis.

We leave for Fort Ellis in the morning at 4 o'clock, in a most splendid "Troy" coach, made by Conn & Ten Broeke, of Chicago, for Mr. L.M. Black, of Bozeman, who kindly sent it over for the use of the party. Our baggage has been transferred this evening, so that we can get off promptly in the morning. General Forsyth found letters here from General Sweitzer and Colonel Gillespie, saying that our camp is already established at Soda Mountain, sixty-five miles from Ellis; and everything is in readiness for our trip to the National Park. A large number of officials and prominent people of the town called upon the Secretary this evening.

Fort Ellis.

July 26.—Left Virginia City at quarter before five, while everything was quiet and still, and moved out in the usual style, every horse on the gallop. The day broke bright and beautiful, and the ride was enjoyed by the party quite as much as the one from Pleasant Valley to Lovells. Immediately upon leaving Virginia City we ascended a lofty mountain, two and a half miles from base to summit, where the view was superb. Directly below us lay the city, seemingly within a stone's throw, surrounded, shut in, and almost hidden by mountain walls. We all took a parting look at the city and the great stretch of country lying to the south over which we have just been traveling; then drove twenty miles to Kirby's on Meadow Creek, for breakfast, making the run in two hours and ten minutes. Breakfast was ready at half-past seven, and it was a repast to remember. I never in my life sat down to a better one, and never expect to, and this opinion was concurred in by every member of the party. Mr. Kirby, who keeps the stage station, and is a graduate of an Eastern College, came here some years since, and now owns a large and valuable stock farm. His wife is a bright-eyed, pleasant, and intelligent lady, and the entire breakfast was cooked by her own hands. The bill of fare was as follows:

Arrival at Fort Ellis

Coffee, with rich, sweet Cream.	Sharp-Tail Grouse, broiled.
Fresh Eggs, soft boiled.	Porter-House Steak.
French Rolls. (Superb.)	Brook Trout.
Corn Bread. (Hard to beat.)	Saratoga Potatoes.
White Bread.	Baked Potatoes.
Brown Bread.	Fresh, delicious Butter.
Milk Toast.	Fresh, rich Milk.
Fricasseed Chickens.	

How is that for a ménu one thousand miles beyond civilization?

Our early morning ride of two hours, and the sharp mountain air, gave us all good appetites, and I can assert without fear of contradiction that justice was done to the viands set before us.

We were soon in motion again, and bowling along at the same reckless speed. Mr. Clark, the Superintendent of the stage and mail line from Virginia City to Bozeman, and from Bozeman to Helena, accompanies us, and handles the reins and whip himself. He may not be as skillful as Lee Goddard, but he is sober, clearheaded, and no mean driver. He said he meant to put us through to Ellis in better style and at a faster pace than we had yet ridden, or would ever again ride in a six-horse coach, and he kept his word, if I may be allowed to judge; besides, he exhibited to us a new feature in stage-driving, which consisted in stoning the leaders, to make them do their part and keep out of the way of the swing horses. At every station where a fresh relay was put in quantities of small stones were thrown on top of the coach, and when the leaders showed the least disposition to shirk their work, a man, sitting on top of the coach, would hurl the projectiles at them, thus keeping a shower of stones flying over Clark's head the greater part of the day.

The scenery all day was grand—mountains on every side, the summits of many white with snow. Our road followed the Madison for twenty-five miles, crossing several lovely valleys, rich with verdure, and almost equal to the great Salt Lake Valley. We took relays of six horses every twelve or fifteen miles, and the animals were all superior ones.

As we gained the summit of the high mountain referred to early this morning, soon after leaving Virginia City, General Marcy remarked that the hill was a "breather"; and the Secretary, somewhat shocked, asked him where he got that expression; so General Marcy had to tell a good story, but, as it is too long to insert here, I refer any one who has the curiosity to hear it to him.

We stopped for supper at the crossing of the west branch of the Gallatin River, eighteen miles from Ellis, where we took our last relay. The coach and horses were here decorated with small flags, and we must have made a gay appearance.

Ten miles out Mr. L. M. Black met us with an elegant turnout, and politely accompanied us into Bozeman. As we came near the town the Silver Cornet Band (a local institution) was playing by the roadside, flags were flying in great profusion, and a salute of seventeen guns was fired in honor of the Secretary's arrival. The reception was certainly very creditable for so small a village. A detachment of Cavalry was also drawn up in the street, ready to escort us on to Fort Ellis. After stopping for a few minutes at Mr. Black's hotel we drove on to the fort, three miles distant, where we were

General R. B. Marcy
Inspector General, U.S.A.

received most cordially by General Sweitzer and his officers, and hospitably assigned to most comfortable quarters.

July 27.—After a late breakfast we passed the forenoon in making the acquaintance of the officers stationed here, and in looking about the post. General Sweitzer, of the Second Cavalry, commands the garrison, which consists of four companies of his own regiment and one company of the Seventh Infantry. The officers and company quarters are comfortable. The post is well laid out, and everything connected with it is kept in good order.

In the afternoon General Marcy, Colonel Gillespie, Captain Ball, and myself went grouse-shooting for two and a half hours, during which we bagged forty-five willow-grouse.

I spent the evening in overhauling my guns and fishing-tackle, and packing up the necessary articles of clothing, & c., for our Yellowstone trip, preparatory to an early start to-morrow morning. The camp equipage, pack-mules, supplies, riding horses, packers, and escort started for Soda Springs three days since. We are to leave at 6 o'clock in ambulances, and expect to drive through to our camp in one day.

Colonel Gillespie gave me to-day a graphic account of the preparations made in Bozeman yesterday to receive the Honorable Secretary of War, in connection with which some amusing incidents occurred. One in regard to the operations of the band is noteworthy, and if space permitted I would give it in the Colonel's own words. When we arrived the town was bright with merry faces; every eye spoke a desire to render homage to the distinguished visitor, and every hand was active in its busy work of preparation. National flags were flying from every available mast, spire, and housetop, and from

27

cords stretched across Main street from roof to roof; conspicuous among these was the tattered flag which General Butler, in 1862, placed over the United States Mint in New Orleans, and for the desecration of which the notorious Mumford paid the penalty of his life. When the Secretary arrived they certainly gave him a warm and generous welcome, and if the execution of the programme was in any way faulty, its conception was noble, heartfelt, and most praiseworthy.

My baggage for the Yellowstone trip consists of one large canvas bag, in which I have packed several colored shirts, two changes of heavy under-clothing, several pairs of heavy socks, a pair of hunting pants, pair of slippers, plenty of handkerchiefs, a light hunting coat, brush and comb, tooth-brush, plenty of towels and soap, mosquito net, rubber pillow, rubber coat, a tin box containing fly-book well filled, reels, lines, and all other necessary fishing tackle. Another box containing rifle implements and many other little things, which go to make up a complete outfit for a fifteen days' camping trip. I take along also one rifle, one shot-gun and case, and a quantity of shells for both; one leather case containing four fishing-rods. I have also a soldier's heavy overcoat, which, with my rubber coat, will be strapped to the cantle of my saddle. I have written a letter home this evening, and have had a dispatch from Chicago, dated yesterday, saying, "All well and everything all right." I am now ready for the Yellowstone Park, and look forward to the trip with intense pleasure.

The Valley of the Yellowstone and The Great National Park.

July 28.—For fifty or sixty years strange and marvelous

stories have been afloat among the hunters and trappers of the Western Territories of a wonderful and mysterious country lying somewhere on the Yellowstone River, near its source, which the Indians never visited, but shunned as the abode of evil spirits; where the rumbling of earthquakes was heard day and night; where volcanoes were to be found, emitting huge columns of boiling hot water; where sulphur and brimstone burst through the ground and flowed in great streams, forming lakes and rivers; where the mountains were rent asunder, creating chasms and cañons thousands of feet in depth; a country where the buffalo, elk, and deer were never seen. These extravagant and absurd stories were told of what this mysterious country contained, but nothing was definitely known about it until 1870.

This remarkable country toward which we are journeying, and about which, until recently, so little has been known, is a huge domain, occupying the northwestern corner of Wyoming Territory, and embracing a region sixty-five miles from north to south and fifty-five miles from east to west, and contains about three thousand five hundred and seventy-five square miles, or two million two hundred and eighty-eight thousand acres.

From the pen of O.B. Bunce, a writer of some note, I copy an account of the first explorations of the Yellowstone Valley, and his brief but graphic description of what it contains:

An exploring party, under Captain Raynolds [incorrectly spelled "Reynolds" in the original journal—R.A.B.] of the United States Engineer Corps, endeavored to enter the Yellowstone Basin in 1859, by way of the Wind River Mountains at the south, but failed on account of the ruggedness of the mountains and the depth of the snow. In 1870 an exploring party, under General Washburn, Surveyor General of Montana, escorted by Lieutenant Gustavus C. Doane, of the Second Cavalry, United States Army, succeeded in entering the valley; and from this source (Doane's report) the public obtained the first trustworthy accounts of the strange land. Immediately thereafter an expedition, under sanction of Congress, was organized by the Secretary of the Interior, and placed in charge of Professor F.V. Hayden, United States Geologist; while, at the same time, a party under command of Captain J.W. Barlow, of the United States Engineer Corps, ascended the Yellowstone and traversed the greater part of the area now included in the Park. Professor Hayden's expedition made a thorough exploration of the whole region, and it is to his full and exhaustive report to Congress that we are indebted for an accurate, detailed knowledge of the strange features of this remarkable land. It is to this gentleman, probably more than to any other person, that we are indebted for the idea of converting the valley into a National Park.

The Yellowstone River, one of the tributaries of the Missouri, has a long, devious flow of thirteen hundred miles ere it loses its waters in those of the larger stream. Its source is a noble lake, situated in Wyoming Territory and nestling amid the snow peaks of the highest mountain range in the country. The upper course of the river is through immense cañons and gorges, and its flow is often marked by splendid water-falls and rapids, presenting, at various points, some of the most remarkable scenery in the country. The entire region about its source is volcanic and abounds in boiling springs, mud volcanoes, soda springs, sulphur mountains, and geysers, the marvels of which outdo those of Iceland.

This remarkable area has recently been set apart by Congress for a great National Park. It certainly possesses striking characteristics for the purpose to which it has been devoted, exhibiting the grand and magnificent in its snow-capped mountains and dark cañons, the picturesque in its splendid water-falls and strangely-formed rocks, the beautiful in the sylvan shores of its noble lake, and the phenomenal in its geysers, hot springs, and mountains of sulphur. It may be claimed that in no other portion of the globe are there united so many surprising features—none where the conditions of beauty and contrast are so calculated to delight the artist, or where the phenomena are so abundant for the entertainment of the student.

Left Ellis at 7 A.M. in two Army ambulances, with four fine mules to each. The Secretary of War and General Marcy occupied one and Generals Forsyth and Sweitzer, Colonel Gillespie and myself the other. A relay of mules had been sent forward to Bottler's Ranch, which point we expected to make about noon.

An escort from the Second Cavalry led off, with instructions to keep from one-half to three-quarters of a mile in advance of us, but always in sight. Indians have been active about Fort Ellis for some weeks, and it was not considered safe to go through to the Yellowstone River without being pretty strong-handed. We were well armed, and had plenty of ammunition. We struck Rock Cañon soon after leaving Ellis, where the scenery was wild and picturesque, with elevated mountains rising above us at many points to the height of a thousand feet or more and well wooded on their northern slopes. For the first five or six miles, or until we reached the Yellowstone Divide, our course was easterly; the road then bore south, and from the summit of the Divide we had a fine view of the Gallatin Valley.

About ten miles from Ellis we struck Trail Creek, which winds through a valley of the same name, leading direct to the Yellowstone. Trail Creek, which we followed for many miles and crossed frequently, is an excellent trout stream, and

I looked at it with longing eyes. After three hours' sharp driving, or about 10 o'clock, we came in sight of the Yellowstone Range, lying to the east of the Yellowstone River, some twenty miles distant. The summit of this, as far as we could see, was covered with snow. Half an hour later we came out of Trail Creek Valley into the great Valley of the Yellowstone. The majestic peaks of the Snow Mountains east of the river, although many miles away, seemed very near, appearing almost to tower above our heads. The Yellowstone, where we struck it, is a wide, deep, swift-running stream; the valley from four to six miles in width; and the river flowing along its eastern side, in many places hugging closely the base or foot-hills of the snow-capped range. Our road, which was now level and smooth, followed the western bank of the river almost due south, crossing several streams flowing into the Yellowstone from the mountain range bordering the valley to the west. We passed a few ranches, but the valley is very little cultivated, although the soil is rich and productive; and should it ever become thickly settled, the numerous streams above alluded to, which flow into the Yellowstone at short intervals, can be used to good advantage for the purposes of irrigation.

Soon after entering the valley the sky became overcast; the wind swept down the valley in strong gusts, and it turned very cold, and soon commenced raining.

At 12:15 P.M. we reached Bottler's, thirty-six miles from Ellis, and half-way to Soda Mountain, where we take a relay of mules. We lunched in Bottler's house, while a garrulous old woman, the mother of the Bottler brothers, kept up an incessant gabble during the few minutes we remained, and was very indignant because we ate our own lunch instead of one she proposed cooking for us, provided we would wait for it. She had a long story to tell in regard to the nice things she had and would cook if we consented to remain, then insisted upon our drinking some wine made from wild berries. The only way we could shake her off was to swallow our lunch quickly and vacate the ranch. The Bottler brothers came here from Iowa, some years since, and have a fine farm. Their wheat and oats, as well as potatoes and other vegetables, were equal to any that can be found in Illinois, Iowa, or Wisconsin. They irrigate their land, of course, taking the water from the mountain streams. Their greatest success, however, has been in raising stock, and in making butter and cheese. We saw in the fields adjoining the house a large number of horses and cattle, many of them fine animals.

The soil of the valley about Bottler's is very fertile. Water, flowing from the mountains, is plentiful everywhere, so that the fields of grain can be irrigated at trifling expense. Bottler told me that the snow rarely fell in the valley, and I am informed that the stock is never sheltered or fed during the severest winters.

The eldest Bottler, Fred., is a mighty hunter, and the trophies of his prowess, such as heads and skins of mountain sheep, elk, deer, bear, and mountain lions are abundant here.

The Valley of the Yellowstone soon after leaving Bottler's begins to contract, and great spurs and ridges extend from the mountains on the west to the Yellowstone River, making it necessary to cross them all at right angles. Each mile we travel to the south finds these rocky spurs higher and rougher. The mountains increase in magnitude as we proceed; the

33

cañons and gorges become deeper and darker; rugged cliffs rise up on every hand; and the river, which a few miles back flowed through level, verdant meadows, now lies buried hundreds of feet below us. The scenery increased in grandeur and sublimity every mile we traveled from Bottler's, and our road led us up one mountain, down another, across a smooth plateau of green grass, then through a cañon and over a mountain peak higher than any we had yet seen, until finally we must have been thousands of feet above the Yellowstone, with now and then a glimpse of it, but appearing to us only a thread from our lofty position. All that I have ever beheld of mountain scenery sinks into utter insignificance by comparison with that we looked upon this afternoon. I do not know, of course, what we are to see further on; at all events, I am prepared for almost anything.

Most of the mountains we have seen to-day are heavily timbered on their peaks and summits, but bare at their base and half-way up the slopes.

Our road from Bottler's was so extremely difficult to follow with ambulances that we were compelled to walk much of the way, and steady the vehicles up and down the sharpest pitches.

Saw great numbers of dusky grouse today, and killed at one point, among the rocky ledges, ten of them with my rifle, without moving three steps, and at another point shot four out of the ambulance. They are a beautiful game-bird, but too tame to afford good sport in shooting; very much like the pinnated grouse in shape and size, but almost black on the breast. General Marcy thinks them the most delicious of all game-birds.

Ten miles from Soda Springs we passed on our right a remarkable freak of nature, known as "Cinnabar Mountain," and the "Devil's Slide." Captain Barlow, in his report, thus describes it:

> The upheaval had carried the strata of which the mountain is formed into a nearly vertical position, with their edges standing out toward the valley, a slight twist or wrench, at the time of the upheaval, giving the strata a curved appearance. Several stand out a hundred feet beyond the general face of the mountain, and extend, probably, a thousand feet upward, leaving rocky depressions between, and giving rise to the name of the "Devil's Slide." There is ample opportunity for him and all his attendants to find amusement here. A deep red tinge, from salts of iron, distinguishes this mountain from all others in its vicinity.

We arrived at Soda Mountain at a quarter to eight, where we found Lieutenant Doane, with the pack train, just going into camp, having been four days reaching this point. The ambulances and wagons go back from here.

Our party is now complete, and is composed of the following persons:

General William W. Belknap, Secretary of War; General Randolph B. Marcy, Inspector General U.S.A.; Colonel George L. Gillespie, Corps of Engineers U.S.A.; General N. B. Sweitzer, of the Second Cavalry; Lieutenant Gustavus C. Doane, Second Cavalry; Assistant Surgeon Robert M. Whitefoot, U.S.A.; and William E. Strong [General James W. Forsyth, U.S.A., was inadvertently absent from the list in the original journal—R.A.B.]. In addition to the above, we have twenty-four enlisted men, selected from Companies, H, F, L, and G, Second Cavalry, the entire party numbering thirty-five persons. Our outfit is the most perfect and complete, for a trip of this kind, that I have ever seen.

We were late in getting our tents pitched and making arrangements for the night. Lieutenant Doane and his packers had a hard day of it, and they were all pretty thoroughly used up when they reached Soda Mountain only a few moments in advance of our party. It was nine o'clock when supper was finally announced, and we were as hungry as wolves, not having had anything to eat but a light lunch since our five o'clock breakfast at Fort Ellis.

The following is the bill of fare of our first supper in camp:

Tomato Soup.	Hot Rolls.
Blue-winged Teal.	Corn Bread.
Dusky Grouse.	Cold White Bread.
Ham and Eggs.	Coffee and Tea, with fresh Cream.
Baked Potatoes.	Fresh Butter.

After supper we sat for a short time around a blazing campfire and smoked our cigars, but were so much fatigued that we went to bed early.

July 29.—Breakfast this morning at 7 o'clock, and as soon as finished we began our final preparations for our long journey on horseback. The saddle-horses were brought out and assigned to members of the party, and to each of us an orderly was directed to report for duty for the trip. We overhauled our baggage for the last time, taking only such things as were deemed absolutely necessary. Our camp at this time presented a busy and exciting scene. The mules were all unbroken to pack-saddles, and some of them, for a long time, objected seriously to having the saddles buckled on them, and when

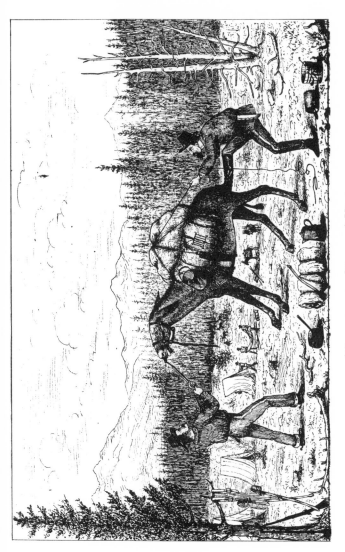

Throwing the Diamond Hitch

this had finally been accomplished, they objected still more seriously to loading on the large packages. They reared, kicked, rolled over, and in some instances broke away from the packers, throwing off their packs. One little white mule behaved so outrageously that it took an hour to conquer him, with four men holding him by the bridle, while four others tried to strap on the pack. He would brace himself and pull straight back, dragging the men in every direction, and when he got tired of this, would swing around in a circle and kick a "blue streak" the moment any one approached him. The pack was finally put on, however, and securely fastened; but the rascal looked as though he would jump off the first precipice he came to, out of sheer spite for the indignities heaped upon him.

General Forsyth and Lieutenant Doane were hard at work till half-past ten in striking the camp and in getting the packs properly made up and thoroughly lashed to the saddles, and in selecting the surplus baggage and supplies to go back by the wagons. Hereafter everything will move easier and smoother. Deducting the nine orderlies, there are fifteen enlisted men, including two or three Sergeants, whose duty it will be to break camp each morning, make up the packs and fasten to the saddles, conduct and look after the train during the day's march, and pitch the tents and arrange camp when the day's march is finished. The men are divided into five or six parties, in charge of a non-commissioned officer, and each party has a special duty assigned it.

About half-past ten the pack-train started out on the trail, and moved off in single file towards the west fork of Gardner's River. Two hours before this, our party on horseback, with orderlies, making quite a cavalcade, left camp with a guide, to look at the first great wonder of the National Park—Soda Mountain Springs.

Soda Mountain Springs, or Mammoth Springs as they are sometimes called, is a great white mountain of soda and magnesia, surmounted by an immense number of boiling springs, which continually send up columns of sulphurous vapor. We saw it for the first time last evening, as we reached the top of the high bluff to the north of our camping-ground, just as daylight was fading away. It appeared like a snow mountain, and the jets of vapor rising from it seemed, in the twilight, like the smoke from the camp-fires of an Army Corps. I should think the base of this mountain occupied an area of two hundred acres—possibly not so much. We rode our horses up a steep ascent on its northeastern slope, a little beyond the point where the overflow begins, and, with our guide, went close up to the Springs, which in some instances cover an eighth to a quarter of an acre. There is great variety in the size, color, and degree of heat of these Springs. Some of them are active, like geysers, and throw up jets of water to the height of two or three feet. Some boil merely, while others are quiet, showing no action whatever, except at the bottom of the basins, where the water pours in through innumerable apertures—bubbles up with a hissing sound—overflows, and rushes along in channels towards the northern and northeastern brink of the mountain, finally spreading out and forming a wide sheet of water, which flows over the mountain's edge, and rushes down its side towards the valley below.

From the base of the mountain, on the plain which stretches out below it, one gets the finest and most satisfactory view of

38

this wonderful system of hot springs. The mountain rises in a gentle slope on the south to the height of two hundred and fifty or three hundred feet; and the whole face or surface of this slope, several hundred feet in width, is beautifully terraced into steps, varying in height from one to ten or twelve feet. Along these terraces, from base to summit, and in regular and systematic order, are thousands of basins of most fantastic form, (the work of centuries, for aught we know). These basins vary in size, but any of them are large enough to bathe in, and have been made by the steady and never-ceasing overflow from the plateaus above. The water flows over the rims of the upper basins into those on the terrace below, and so on to the bottom, and is composed of magnesia, lime, and sulphur, and as it issues from the springs on the summit is so hot that I could not bear my hand in it. A person wishing to bathe here can select a basin of any size or shape to suit his fancy. The edges and outer rims of many of the smaller basins are beautifully colored—pink, blue, and yellow predominating, and the incrustations on the sides and bottoms are exquisite in design.

Nearly all visitors to the Mammoth Springs bathe in these scalloped basins; and, as the temperature of the pools varies from sixty to two hundred degrees, they have no difficulty in selecting the temperature that suits them best. Captain Barlow says "a few of these springs are strongly mineral, but most of them are sufficiently pure for drinking and cooking purposes."

At the foot of Soda Mountain, and within a few feet of the lower terrace, is a defunct conical geyser called "Liberty Cap," which is fifty or sixty feet in height, with a large opening at the top.

The surface of this Mountain, in the vicinity of the Springs, where we traversed it on horseback and on foot, seemed but a thin crust, which caused us all to be cautious in our investigations and none of us cared to examine very minutely, although our guide seemed to think there was no danger and walked anywhere, without the slightest hesitation. I must confess, however, that I was very glad to get off this Mountain with my horse.

We visited the Grotto, the Devil's Kitchen, and the Great Cave, all places of interest and well worth seeing, and at half-past ten o'clock descended the Mountain, taking the trail for the Yellowstone Basin—distant thirty-six miles—which was very well defined, but narrow and in places difficult to follow on horseback, so that we had frequently to dismount and lead our horses.

We soon reached and crossed Gardner's River in safety; although the water was quite deep, the bottom rocky and extremely rough, and the current so strong that the horses were nearly carried off their feet. A mile further on we reached and crossed the east fork of Gardner's River, and entered the Grand Cañon, which was grand indeed. Words are weak to fitly describe the magical beauty of this lovely gorge. Our trail began at the very bottom, with a gradual ascent at first; but the grade increased as we gained the middle of the cañon, where the trail was only from ten to twelve inches in width, and cut out most of the way from the side of a precipitous wall, which rose vertically on our left hand to a great height.

Gardner's River was at our feet, at first a dashing, foaming mountain torrent; and, as we worked up towards the top, the cañon below us grew deep and deeper, until the stream faded and disappeared in the dizzy chasm. Higher and higher we ascended the trail, winding in and out, following closely the face of this rocky cañon, now and then crossing a spur or isolated ledge that fairly hung over this frightful abyss, so that we seemed at times suspended in mid-air. Once I turned my head and looked back towards Soda Mountain. The view was superb, but I felt no disposition to repeat it. My eyes were fixed on the face of the rocky wall to my left, while the scene to my right had but little attraction to me at this particular juncture.

As we drew near the head of the cañon, where the trail turns suddenly to the right, Gardner's Falls burst upon us. It was a beautiful picture from where we saw it. A dense forest of pine and balsam fairly hemmed in and shut off from view the river above the Falls, hiding all but the final leap. The water appeared to rush out from a dense mass of green foliage, making its jump of one hundred and twenty-five feet to the bed of the river below.

Emerging from this dangerous cañon we gained the smooth, grassy plain at the summit of the range, and facing our horses to the rear, enjoyed for some moments the panorama of the cañon we had just conquered and the grand stretch of mountain scenery beyond, then galloped on over a rolling prairie, thickly covered with wild flowers of rare beauty, with here and there little groves of balsam, cedar, and spruce, through which our trail led us. The day was charming; we were all in good spirits, and enjoyed to the highest degree the magnificent scenery which lay spread out on every hand.

We reached Black-Tail Deer Creek at 4 P. M., having been

four hours on the road and traveled but eight miles. Doane thought we had better camp here as none of the pack-mules were yet in sight, and, as it was the first day out, the mules would hardly make any greater distance. This proved true, as none of the pack animals got in till late, and two or three were out after midnight.

Black-Tail Deer Creek is quite celebrated as a trout stream, and we looked for fine fishing. Got out the rods immediately upon our arrival and went to work, but had poor success. There seemed to be plenty of small trout, but they were very shy. Tried fancy flies of every sort, but failed to entice them, and finally caught grasshoppers for bait, but had no better success, only taking sufficient for supper and breakfast. The whole country is swarming with grasshoppers that drop by hundreds into the stream, and the fish are undoubtedly surfeited with food. Doane went back to meet the pack-train soon after we halted, and came up with the mules bearing our mess-chests and tents at 5 P.M. The remainder of the pack animals were far back, and the packers have had great trouble. The new pack cords and straps continued to stretch, and many of the packs became disarranged, slipped on the saddles, turned over, and two of them broke, the contents rolling down the Great Cañon. One of the mules (not the white one) slipped on the trail and rolled off the precipice, severely bruising the packer in charge, but the mule luckily caught on some rocks and was saved.

Our supper was rather late, but after we had finished, Doane and myself mounted our horses and rode over the grand plateau to the foot-hills to try and get a deer. We saw three black-tails, but it was too dark to shoot at or follow them,

Lieutenant Gustavus C. Doane
Second Cavalry, U.S.A.

and we returned to camp about 8 o'clock, finding a cheerful camp-fire burning, around which we sat for some time, smoking and chatting.

General Forsyth's stock of stories still holds out, and I am inclined to think he reserved his best for the Yellowstone country. The Secretary and General Marcy are still able to tell some good ones. General Sweitzer, Colonel Gillespie, Lieutenant Doane, and Doctor Whitefoot are all capital traveling companions, and the time passes quickly and pleasantly.

Lieutenant Doane, who is the guide for our party, and who has charge of the pack-train and the management of the men, is a striking officer. Tall, straight as an arrow, very dark complexion, with black hair and a long, sweeping, dark mustache, he would certainly attract attention in any company. This is his fourth trip to the Park, and he is perfectly familiar with it and knows more about the wonders it contains than anybody. In this country he is spoken of and pointed out as the man who "invented Wonderland." When his report was published, by authority of Congress, soon after his exploration with General Washburn in 1870, it was not believed by many. By others it was thought to be grossly overdrawn, but the subsequent reports of Professor Hayden, Barlow, and Jones proved that it was impossible for any one to exaggerate the wonders of the Great Geyser Basin or the beauties of the Grand Cañon of the Yellowstone. Doane is a superb horseman, a keen and daring hunter, and a dead shot. We are very fortunate to have him with us on this trip.

July 30.—Breakfasted at 5:30 and broke camp at 6 o'clock. The packs were made up and strapped to the saddles in an incredibly short space of time. The white mule skulked and kicked some, but was finally forced to terms and submitted gracefully at last. All the other mules were quiet as kittens. The orders are, to have our breakfast every morning at half-past five and to be in the saddle at six, the pack-train to follow on as soon as possible.

The party moved on the direct trail to Tower Falls or Tower Creek, where we camp to-night; but General Marcy and myself resolved to have a deer hunt, and branched off with our orderlies in the same direction and over the same ground traveled by Doane and myself last night. It was our intention to strike the trail some time during the day, six or eight miles from camp. Soon after leaving our party we separated, General Marcy bearing off to the south and west, aiming for the summit of the Snowy Range, which lay before us. We agreed to meet, later in the day, on one of the high peaks to the south, and General Marcy pointed out the particular spot, which was well-marked, and we agreed upon the hour.

I hunted faithfully along Black-Tail Deer Creek to near its source, skirting along the edge of the wooded ravines, sometimes on foot and sometimes on horseback, crept to the summit of the prominent ridges, cautiously and silently, sometimes leading my horse by the bridle-rein and again leaving him behind in charge of my orderly, expecting every moment to start an elk or deer, but game was scarce. I saw at one time two deer on an open plain, five hundred yards away, but they discovered me at the same time. I tried every device to get near enough for a shot, but failed, and they finally disappeared in a wooded ravine, half a mile distant to the left and rear. About 10 o'clock I began the ascent of the mountain to meet

44

General Marcy. It was a long and tedious journey, but after some desperate climbing, I accomplished it, and stood on the very spot, as I supposed, designated by Marcy in the morning. How refreshing it was! A strong breeze swept over the crest, and, although warmly dressed, I fairly shivered with the cold. Banks of snow all around and beneath me, and in the upper end of the gorges which cut into the great range, where I was standing, the snow was packed, seemingly, to an immense depth. The silence was almost painful; not a sound to be heard except the wind and the swaying of the pines and balsams with which I was surrounded. Way below me, hundreds of feet, sailing and soaring above and around a bare and isolated peak, was an eagle; no other bird in sight, and I saw no game or forest birds during the entire day. I swept the open country in every direction with my field-glass for nearly two hours, but General Marcy was not to be seen, and at length I gave it up, and commenced the descent, which I found more difficult than going up. Finally we reached the foot-hills and the margin of the great plateau, where I continued to hunt for game, at the same time keeping an eye out for General Marcy. There was no danger of getting lost, as the whole country below the base of the mountains and hills was open, with wooded ravines and little groves scattered about. I could see to the east the Snowy Mountain Range, which ran to the south, and I knew the Yellowstone River flowed along its base, and if I struck due east, I would certainly find the trail. I hunted till 1 o'clock faithfully, but seeing no game or signs of game, and hearing or seeing nothing of Marcy, concluded I had better look for the trail and work towards camp, which was twelve or fifteen miles away. I found the trail with but little difficulty, and struck out briskly for camp, suffering so much from soreness that I was compelled to dismount and lead my horse the greater part of the way to camp. Not having been on horseback for nine years, I rode too fast and too far for the first day. Yesterday's ride I do not count, as we only traveled eight miles. The horse I have is an excellent one, gentle, easy-gaited, a fast walker and sure-footed. Like all Cavalry horses, he is broken to trot, but think I can make him gallop after a day or two.

Reached camp at 6 o'clock, most thoroughly used up. Found tents pitched and supper nearly ready. General Marcy got into camp before me. He had been looking for me the best part of the day. Probably I went too far up the mountain, or missed the rendezvous altogether. I must have been in fault, as General Marcy is too old a mountaineer to have gone astray. Neither of us killed anything or fired a shot, and the General saw no game or fresh sign. Lieutenant Doane says the elk and deer at this season are on the highest mountain ranges, where the snow lies all the year, to escape flies and mosquitoes. We have seen no elk as yet, and I am sure we were high enough up to-day.

I missed the trail, four miles from camp, or rather took the wrong trail, and brought up at Baronette's Cabin, between two forks of the Yellowstone. Crossed the west branch on a good bridge made by Baronette in the winter of 1870, soon after Doane made his first trip to the Yellowstone Valley. I rested here for a time, when Baronette kindly accompanied me back, and put me on the right trail to Tower Falls. He had just returned from our camp, and says he will meet our party seven or eight days hence at Yellowstone Lake; and if

General Marcy and I want a hunt such as we have never had, he will give it to us without fail. His plan is, for us to cross the Yellowstone, near the Lake, swimming our horses, and hunt about Pelican Creek, returning to his cabin on the east side of the Yellowstone River, and meeting the party en route for Ellis. As this will give us three or four days among the grizzlies, elk, and black-trailed deer, nothing would please me better. Baronette says there is very little game to the west of the Yellowstone, and that we have a slender prospect of killing anything but grouse.

To the east of the Yellowstone, and particularly between his cabin and the head of the Yellowstone Lake, including the Pelican Creek country, big game is still so very abundant that he says we will see elk in great bands, containing hundreds, and no end to mountain sheep and deer.

Baronette, or "Jack Baronette," as he is best known, is a celebrated character in this country, and although famous as an Indian fighter and hunter, he is still more celebrated as a guide. His knowledge of the mountains, rivers, and trails of the Western Territories is very extensive, as he has traveled over the greater part of California. From early boyhood he has lived in the mountains, and his whole life is a chapter replete with adventure and hair-breadth escapes. When Mr. Everts was lost on Doane's expedition, in 1870, and wandered for thirty-seven days among the mountains and cañons of the Yellowstone, living on roots, wild berries, and grasshoppers, Jack Baronette found him, on the fifteenth day, brought him in, and saved his life. He is highly esteemed by those who know him, and his word is as good as gold. He is of medium stature, broad shouldered, very straight, and built like Longfellow's ship, for "strength and speed"; eyes black as a panther's and as keen and sharp; complexion quite dark, with hair and whiskers almost black. He speaks well, using good English, and his manner is mild, gentle, and modest, is proud of his knowledge of the mountains and of his skill with the rifle. I took to him at once, and before he left me at the Tower Falls trail we had become good friends. I must have a hunt with Jack Baronette before we leave the National Park.

Immediately after my arrival in camp I took a cold bath in Tower Creek, and felt much refreshed. Tower Creek, just below the falls, is famous for its great trout. I arrived too late to fish, but the party caught some magnificent strings— running from two and a half to four pounds. General Forsyth and Colonel Gillespie had the best success of any of the party. Forsyth used a sixteen ounce fly-rod and a brown hackle fly. I hope we will camp here on our return trip, so that I can have a chance to hook a four-pounder—something I have never yet done.

Our camp to-night is charming. Tents are pitched in a sharp bend of the river just above the falls and within a stone's throw of it. The creek sweeps entirely around us in a graceful curve, and fifty yards below leaps in a single bound over a fall of one hundred and fifty-six feet. The background is a bluff, rising one hundred feet above us, with dense growth of pine and spruce, at the base of which is our camp, with a blazing fire in front of tents, and around which we all gather with our cigars, as soon as supper is over. The story-tellers were all in good humor and we had some good ones. It took General Marcy some time to kill four grizzlies and get them into camp, and Doane could not kill nine mountain sheep while the band was rushing by, and dress and hang them up in less than five minutes. The stories told by the Secretary, Generals Forsyth and Sweitzer, not being sportsmen, were of a different character, but none the less enjoyable. I never passed a pleasanter evening in my life around a camp-fire.

Tower Falls and Tower Creek.

Tower Creek comes in from the west and flows into the Yellowstone three and a half miles from Baronette's. It is rapid, but not deep. The Fall is the great curiosity; the water rushes with a tremendous current over a rugged, rocky face, and is precipitated in an unbroken sheet into the bed of the gorge below, and a few hundred yards further on, the stream mingles its waters with those of the Yellowstone.

The view of the Falls and the cañon, as seen from the eastern bank near our camp, was very picturesque and beautiful. Great pinnacles of rock rise up on either side near the crest of the Falls to the height of one hundred feet or more. Pines, spruce, and balsam stretch along the tops of the hills on both sides forming the crest of the cañon, and, below, the vertical walls are seamed and scarred very strangely, and half-way down they narrow up so that the sunlight is almost excluded. I did not descend the cañon, but others of the party did, and from this description I should judge the view must be much grander than from above.

July 31.—Breakfast promptly at the hour fixed, and in the saddle at 6. Members of the party pretty generally complain of being lame and sore. I was hardly able to sit in my saddle when we first mounted, but improved gradually during the day.

49

Two days more will, undoubtedly, see us all well broken in and able to ride almost any distance. The saddle-horses are all fine ones, but the Secretary's is the most beautiful animal of all.

General Marcy killed some dusky grouse soon after leaving camp. Our trail led directly towards Mount Washburn, over the numerous spurs which shot out from the main peak. The ascent was very gradual, and for a long distance the trail followed a narrow ridge which finally brought us nearly abreast of the highest peak, some distance to the left of the trail.

The party was unanimous in the desire to scale this lofty peak, as from its summit the Yellowstone Basin and all the wonders it contains can be seen. Doane said we could ride our horses to the very top, so after a brief halt we began the ascent. At first it was easy work enough, but it soon became very difficult for horses and riders. Higher and higher we climbed, and peak after peak we gained and passed, but still the main objective point was further on. The higher we got the more precipitous the peaks, until we could not ascend in a direct line, but described great circles and zig-zag courses. The smaller ranges and peaks which we passed were wholly destitute of timber, but the little valleys intervening, and the slopes of the hills which rose one above the other in regular succession and at short intervals, were rich with verdure and decked with flowers of every hue. Springs of pure water bubbled out from rocky crevices and flowed across our path, but in almost every instance the surface of the mountain streams was frozen, and often the ice was strong enough to bear horse and rider. As incomprehensible as it may appear, banks of snow, frozen streams, grass, and flowers were here found side by side.

Tired and breathless we gained the summit of Mount Washburn, and in an instant of time, without the faintest warning, the whole grand panorama burst upon us. At our feet, as it were, lay spread out for our inspection the mysterious country we have come so far to see. "Wonderland" (as it is called in Montana) was before and below us; and right by our side and slightly in advance stood the man who first discovered it all, and who wrote the first report of its mountains and valleys, its geysers and cañons, its lakes and water-falls. Hayden and Barlow and Jones have examined it, all officially, and their reports are exhaustive, scientific, and most interesting; but Doane saw it first, wrote the first report, and brought it all to the notice and attention of the world. Give him the credit.

Grand, glorious, and magnificent was the scene as we looked upon it from Washburn's summit. No pen can write it—no language describe it. Long we gazed upon the picture before a word was spoken, and then, when one after another broke out in expressions of admiration, Doane pointed out the objects of greatest interest. We were eleven thousand feet above the level of the sea, and two thousand feet above the Yellowstone Basin, which is nearly circular in form, and from fifty to sixty miles in diameter. To the south and east lay Yellowstone Lake, nestled snugly at the base of snow-capped mountains, its broad, blue sheet of water distinctly visible, although twenty-six miles away. In the dim distance, and one hundred and twenty-six miles to the southwest, were the snowy tops of the three Great Tetons on Snake River, rising thirteen thousand five hundred feet above the sea level, and the highest peaks in that range of the Rocky Mountains. At our left, and but a few miles from us, was the Grand Cañon of the Yellowstone, the face of its eastern wall for two hundred feet in plain view; and Doane pointed out the exact locality of the Lower Falls and the Geyser Basins.

On every side of us were mountain peaks above mountain peaks; range above range, in endless succession, snow-capped, most of them, but some bare and brown from base to summit, and others wooded on slope and peak, the dark green of pine, spruce, and balsam forming a rich contrast with the white and brown; great smooth plateaus and rolling prairies, dotted with groves and sparkling with running streams—the whole forming a landscape wild, beautiful, and picturesque, and surpassing in grandeur anything I ever looked upon.

The wind blew a gale while we remained on the summit, and we were all thoroughly chilled before we left. General Forsyth found in a bottle, under some loose rocks, the cards of several parties who had ascended Washburn before us; one with the names of General Sweitzer, Lieutenant Doane, and three or four other officers, who made the ascent in 1871; also the cards of Lord Dunraven and his party, who were here in 1874. Forsyth wrote the names of our party, with date (July 31, 9 A.M.), on half a sheet of note-paper, which was deposited in a small tin box, and placed it with the other cards under the rock.

We gained the summit at nine, and at quarter to ten commenced the dangerous descent. Crossing a narrow gorge, to the east of Washburn, we struck an adjoining range, which we followed for some distance, then commenced descending the southern slope. For a time we rode, but soon were forced to dismount and lead our horses. Doane still led and our cav-

General James W. Forsyth
United States Army

alcade followed on in single file, but at length began to scatter, each one selecting his own route. The steep and smooth side of the mountain made it extremely difficult and at times impossible for horses or men to maintain their footing. Such slipping and sliding among loose rocks, such holding on and bracing back, I never witnessed. Sometimes we were pulling at the bridle-reins to get our horses along, and again the horses were dragging us, in spite of every exertion. Occasionally a great bowlder, loosened by some one above and behind, would come dashing down like a rifled cannon-shot, threatening death and destruction to those in advance, and there was sharp dodging all along the line to avoid them down this mountain's side for two thousand feet, but we finally reached the valley in safety, barring scratches and torn clothes, and I can safely assert that none of us would care to repeat the performance under any circumstances. After resting thoroughly we again mounted our horses, and, led by Doane, struck across the valley to view the Grand Cañon. We soon reached it, and from several points had fine views of its rocky walls, hundreds of feet down. The ragged edges of the chasm, Doane says, are from two hundred to five hundred yards apart, and the walls are two thousand feet straight down to the bed of the stream. From no point could we see the river. It was entirely lost and buried in this frightful abyss. No sounds came up, but a deathly stillness prevailed everywhere in this vicinity. This cañon is so deep, dark, and awful that one is well satisfied to inspect it at a safe distance. We spent half an hour at the cañon, then struck for the main trail leading to the Lower Falls, stopping on the way to look at the Sulphur Springs, which are curious and interesting—great vats, from six to twenty feet in diameter, of boiling sulphur, which are fitly called the "Devil's Caldrons." The odor arising from them was sickening. Many of these springs were very active, and cast up columns of boiling sulphur and jets of hot water to the height of several feet. We rode our horses quite near to many of them, then moved on towards camp, looking for the trail, which Doane missed, and for two or three hours could not recover. The woods were fearful to travel through, covered with a small growth of pine, from six to eight inches in diameter, but standing so thick and close that our horses could, at times, barely squeeze through; and add to this a perfect labyrinth of fallen timber, with limbs and branches entwined in every imaginable shape, and some idea can be formed of the difficulties which beset us. Several times the horses were checked and the party dismounted, while Doane reconnoitred for the trail, but was unsuccessful in his search, and at length decided we must continue on in a more westerly course. The members of the party were tired out, and the delay was anything but agreeable. The Secretary and General Forsyth were annoyed and disgusted at the way Doane led us, but said little. Doane seems to have the most magnificent contempt for a trail, and will leave it at any moment to dash straight across the country, no matter how rough and difficult, if he thinks anything is to be saved in distance.

Soon after starting on our westerly course, and while passing along the border of a great marsh or meadow, a strange animal was discovered coming towards us from the west. It resembled a wolf, only the body appeared longer and it had a tremendous tail, which was white. It came prancing along through the grass, unconscious of our presence, frequently springing into the air, as though trying to catch something. The party halted under cover of the wood bordering the southern margin of the marsh, while I dismounted, rifle in hand, and ran rapidly towards him, crouching as low as possible in the grass. For some time the animal came directly towards me, but finally changed his course and headed for the timber. Thinking I could get no nearer, I fired at him while running, at full four hundreds yards. The ball must have gone close, for he stopped instantly, raised on his hind legs, and looked straight at me. I fired again, taking as careful and accurate aim as I was capable, but the ball went astray. He now seemed to wake up and appreciate fully the situation, for he broke for the timber directly opposite from me. I fired at him again while running, and this time with better success, for he sprang high into the air, and the next instant was rolling over and over, and struggling and kicking in the grass. The party shouted "You have killed him," and I really thought I had, and proceeded quite leisurely towards the animal, having lost my breath from my run across the marsh. I had not traveled a hundred yards from the point where I fired last when I saw my game disappearing in the edge of the wood, but from his actions evidently mortally wounded. I fired at him three times in quick succession, but could not tell whether I struck him or not. Rushing quickly to the point in the woods where I saw him last, I found the trail covered with blood, and followed it for three or four hundred yards, every moment expecting to find the animal dead. I was, however, disappointed. The trail soon led into a densely-wooded ravine, and as the day was far advanced, the party tired out, and a trail yet to be found, I gave up the chase. I am very confident, however, that the animal was fatally shot, and that I would have found him soon had I kept to the trail. The animal was a wolverine, and is very rarely found in this country. General Marcy says he never saw but one in his life, and that he wounded at a long distance, and it escaped in almost precisely the same manner as the one to-day. Doane never killed one, but saw one in the Park on his first expedition.

Half an hour afterwards Doane struck the trail over which most of the pack-train had passed, and at 3 o'clock we reached the Great Falls.

The Falls of the Yellowstone.

Niagara is grander, more sublime, and more impressive. The Niagara River, about the Falls and Suspension Bridge, is three times the size of the Yellowstone; but take the Falls of the Yellowstone, with the cañon, just below the lower leap, and the view one gets, even from above, surpasses in beauty a dozen Niagaras. I think no one but Doane, accompanied by a private soldier, has ever descended the Grand Cañon below the Falls.

After viewing the Falls and Cañon for an hour, we proceeded to our camp on Cascade Creek, which we reached at half-past four. The camp is lovely, and plenty of good grazing. The last of the pack-train came in at 5:30, having made eighteen miles over a rough trail. We have had a hard day on horseback, and are so used up that we will not probably sit around the camp-fire very late to-night.

When our party descended Mount Washburn this morning Colonel Gillespie galloped ahead with his orderly, thinking

Colonel George L. Gillespie
Corps of Engineers, U.S.A.

we would follow at once. Saw no more of him until we got to camp. We were considerably alarmed about him when his absence from the party was noted, which was about the time we left the valley at the base of Washburn. It is easy to get lost in this country, and few people would dare to leave the trail, under any circumstances, without an experienced guide, like Doane or Baronette. Gillespie, however, galloped on without the slightest hesitation, visited the Grand Cañon, the Sulphur and Mud Springs, and the Fall, and got to camp two hours before us. I think it very remarkable. General Marcy could probably have done the same, but not one person in a thousand could.

The grouse General Marcy shot this morning we had for supper. I agree that the dusky-grouse is the finest for the table of any of the grouse family—meat white, tender, and juicy.

August 1.—Very cold last night, and the three blankets and an overcoat which I had over me were insufficient to keep me comfortable. When we dressed, at 5 o'clock, the ground was white with frost, and water froze last night in buckets outside our tents to the thickness of half an inch.

We took another look at the Lower Falls, and the Grand Cañon below, this morning. We also viewed the cañon from Moran's Point, which was named for Moran, the artist, and from which point he painted the picture now in the House of Representatives. Doane took us to a point half a mile below the Lower Falls, where we got a superb view of it. We crept slowly down the sloping bank of the cañon, holding on to light sapling pines and protruding points of rocks, and finally came to an isolated spur or ledge, which shot out and overhung the cañon. The back of this spur, seven to eight feet in width, was carpeted with grass, and on the extreme end a mass of irregular rocks, five or six feet in height, rose up, forming a breastwork convenient to lean against or cling to, and two or three stunted pines sprang up from its base, which we were glad to make use of. Doane went out first, and the others followed one at a time. It seemed as though we were walking a tight-rope as we passed over this spur, seven or eight feet wide, and I could not divest myself of the feeling that at the next step the whole ledge would go down with us into the yawning chasm. We thus obtained a full, unobstructed view of the Falls from the rocks at the end of the spur, and this is the only place where a perfect view can be had. We were here fairly suspended over the cañon, and the Yellowstone went dashing madly by, almost beneath us, and only one thousand and fifty feet away. It was a giddy height and a fearful position we occupied; and notwithstanding the grandeur and unsurpassed beauty of the Falls, river, and cañon, I was happy when the slope of the cañon was regained, and happier still when the bank was reached.

As we came out of camp in the early morning and reached the high ground north of Cascade Creek, the scene far to the south in the geyser basins attracted our attention for some moments. The vapor and steam from the volcanoes, geysers, and boiling springs were rising up, like smoke from the camp-fires of an army. There was no wind, and the columns of steam rose perpendicularly to a great height. The morning was cold, the air fresh and bracing, like an early day in November. The grass and flowers on the plateau and in the woods between our camping-ground and the mouth of Cascade Cañon were white and glistening with frost. Later, when the sun got higher and the frost melted, the flowers looked fresher and brighter than ever.

The next point of interest beyond the Falls is the "Seven Sisters" (Sulphur Springs), which we reached at half-past ten. They consist of seven distinct round-topped hills or mounds, in one group, all covered with sulphur springs, varying in size and temperature. These springs are very similar to the "Devil's Caldrons" at the base of Washburn, only larger and more active. The basin of one was seventeen by twenty-two feet in diameter. After spending some time here we passed on to our camp at the Mud Volcanoes, which lie within three hundred yards of the Yellowstone, having made fourteen miles with pack-train and our party having ridden over twenty. We are all getting over our soreness, and have stood the horseback ride of to-day exceedingly well.

The country lying along our trail to-day has been tame and uninteresting compared with the stretch of country between Ellis and the Falls. The trail follows closely the Yellowstone, which is so changed one hardly recognizes it; no falls, foaming rapids, or cañons, but a broad, smooth, placid river, with a slow, steady current, and banks level, in many places rising but a few inches above the water's surface.

Our lunch was finished at 1 o'clock, and I at once got out my case of fishing-rods and fly-book, and with my orderly, Flynn, took the shortest route to the river. I had heard such stories of the fabulous size of the trout in the Yellowstone that I was very eager to try my hand. The moment I reached the bank I could see them in immense numbers everywhere in the stream, and they were certainly large enough to satisfy the aspirations of the most ardent and enthusiastic fisherman. The stream where I struck it was very rapid, and full of little eddies. Near the shore the water was more quiet and clear as crystal, wherein hundreds of trout could be seen swimming and darting swiftly up and down the current, but near the bottom. Selecting my lightest fly-rod, my reel and line were soon attached, and I put on a six-foot leader and three flies—a gray professor at the end of the leader and two brown hackles above. In the meantime I had kept well back from the river bank, and now being ready I grasped the rod firmly in my right hand, crept cautiously up to the proper distance, and made my first cast into the Yellowstone. The wind was in my favor and the flies went well out, touching lightly the water's surface. The trout were there, I knew, and I expected to hook one the instant the flies struck, but I was doomed to disappointment—there was no response. I drew in my line quietly and gently and cast again, but with no better result. Again and again I threw out the line until my arm was tired, but the trout refused to rise to a fly. I thereupon began experimenting by putting on a shorter leader, with two flies attached, then used but one; and finally I tried every color in my book, but to no purpose. Thus I spent an hour without a single rise, and at length gave it up. "Flynn," said I, "catch grasshoppers," and in five minutes he had a tin-box full. Taking off my leader, I fastened to the line a brilliant fly, which Mr. Walker, of Chicago, gave me two years ago, and put on the hook a grasshopper for bait and three buckshot for sinkers, just above the snell. A short distance above the place where I had been casting was a great rock, six feet square and about four feet from shore. It was but a short jump from the bank, and I was quickly on it. Just here the river made a sharp bend, and the water was so rapid and turbulent that the fish were hidden from my new position.

My First Trout in the Yellowstone.

Again I threw out my hook in the swift water, and down the stream it went like lightning, tossing about like a feather in the rapids. My reel whirled and spun like a buzz-saw, the line went out so fast. I never touched the reel to check the running line till seventy-five feet, at least, was in the water, then I pressed my thumb firmly upon it and drew gently back the rod. At the same instant something struck my hook that nearly carried me off my feet, and I had to let go the reel to save the rod. I had him fast, securely hooked, but could I land him? That was the question. I gave him twenty-five or thirty feet more line, then checked again and tried to hold him, but it was no use, the rod bent nearly double, and I had to let him run. My line was one hundred and fifty feet in length, and I knew when it was all out, if the fish still kept in the rapids, I should lose him. No tackle like mine could stand for a moment against the strength of such a fish as I had struck and in such swift water. I therefore continued to give him the line, but no faster than I was forced to, until no more than twelve or fifteen feet remained upon the reel, when, fortunately for me, he turned to the left and was carried into an eddy which swept him into more quiet water near the shore. Twice in his straight run down the rapid current of the stream he leaped clear from the water, and I saw he was immense—something double or triple the size of any trout I had ever caught. The excitement to me was greater than anything I had ever experienced. No one but a trout fisherman can understand or appreciate the intense pleasure of that single run. I was crazy to kill and land him, and yet I knew the chances were against it. For ten minutes I played the trout as skillfully as I knew how. Again and again I reeled him up within twenty-five or thirty feet of the rock, but he was game to the last, and would dart off with the same strength as when first struck, and I had to let him go. Finally he showed signs of exhaustion; and I managed to get him to the top of the water, and then worked him in close to the shore, where Flynn was waiting to take the line and throw him out, as I had no landing net. Flynn did it very well. Watching his opportunity, when the trout was very near the bank and quiet, he lifted him out. He was a fine specimen, and would weigh four pounds if he would weigh an ounce. I estimated his weight from the large trout which I have taken from Thunder Lake and Thunder River, on the Upper Peshtigo, and which weigh from one pound to one pound and a quarter, with now and then one reaching one pound and a half, but none larger than that. This trout was three times the size of any I ever caught on the Peshtigo or anywhere else. At 4:30 o'clock I stopped fishing, having landed thirty-five trout, which would run from two and a half to four and a half pounds in weight, none less than two and a half pounds; and I must have struck from seventy-five to one hundred of these immense fish. I am sure I lost more than I landed. A dozen hooks at least were broken and several times my line was carried away above the snell; besides, Flynn lost at least fifteen in landing. I never saw a finer string of trout in my life; my orderly had strung them on a forked branch of willow, and the only way we could get the string to camp was by dragging them upon the ground, Flynn taking one side of the branch and I the other. Such fishing I never had before, and I would have given a great deal if Mr. George Walker, Mr. Johnston, and the other members of our Thunder Lake party were here to enjoy this unequaled sport.

While I was fishing, the Secretary, General Forsyth, and Colonel Gillespie came down to the river and watched me and a number of soldiers who were fishing at the same time above and below us, the men using a short stiff pole, a great, heavy line, and large hook; and the moment the trout took the bait they jerked them straight out. Not much science in that kind of angling, I should imagine, but they got them much faster than a person with light tackle, such as I was using. A man standing near me threw out at one time, four very large fish while I was playing one, which I finally lost. I do not know how many fish were caught this afternoon by the entire party, but several hundred I am sure. Soon after I reached camp with my trout General Marcy came in with an immense string he had taken a mile or so above our camp; quite as many on his string as mine, and averaging larger if anything. From his account he must have had equally as good sport as myself. Although these fish made good play, they would not rise to a fly, but would jump for a grasshopper the moment it struck the water. In the excitement of landing a trout the General, in some way, fell into the river, and got thoroughly drenched; I think the bank gave way and let him in, or else he slipped on a root. Instead of returning to camp and changing his wet clothes, he remained for two hours and more, and when he finally got in was shaking like a person with the ague—very imprudent, it seems to me, for a man of his venerable years and experience. Hope he will not suffer from it.

After dinner General Forsyth and I went down to the river again with our rods, and fished till after dark. Our orderlies built a great bonfire on the river's bank, and the trout took our hooks freely until nearly 9 o'clock, so that we were very successful, and caught more trout than we could carry or lift. General Forsyth does not pretend to be much of a hunter, but he is certainly a superb, enthusiastic fisherman. I think we would have fished all night if the trout had continued to bite.

The Mud Volcano.

Captain Barlow's description of the Mud Volcano and the springs which surround it is given in his official report, and will be far more interesting to the reader than any description that I could possibly write. I quote from his report:

The central point of interest here is the Mud Volcano, which has broken out from the side of a well-timbered hill. It has a crater twenty-five feet across at the top, gradually sloping inward to the bottom, where it becomes about half this diameter. Its depth is about thirty feet. The deposit is gray mud, nearly a pure alumina, and has been thrown up by the action of the volcano at no very distant period. The rim of the crater, on the down-hill side, is some ten feet in height, and trees fifty feet high and one hundred feet distant are loaded with mud thrown from this volcano. The surface of the bottom is in a constant state of ebullition, puffing and throwing up masses of boiling mud, and sending forth dense columns of steam several hundred feet above the surrounding forests. This column of steam can be seen for many miles in all directions.

Our camp was pitched near the large volcano, and as it is the first genuine geyser we have seen we watched it with great interest. It has been in full play three times since we arrived, at 2, at 4, and at 10 o'clock.

We move to-morrow morning for the great geyser basins which lie directly to the west and beyond the great divide between the Madison and Yellowstone Rivers. Will leave the larger part of our camp equipage, mess outfit, and supplies here, taking only five days' rations, the wall-tent for the Secretary and General Marcy, and tent-fly for the rest of the party. We will only take ten pack-mules to transport what we absolutely need. We are forced to go in light marching order and rough it to some extent, as the trail is said to be very difficult. The main camp, with the supplies, will be moved from this point to Yellowstone Lake, where we join it upon our return.

August 2.—Were late in leaving camp this morning, but got off finally at 7 o'clock, pack-train one hour behind us. Had no trail, but the general direction was west.

General Marcy complained of not feeling well this morning, and he certainly looks badly. He was in no condition to travel, but nothing could keep him back. Ten minutes after we left camp and came to prairie land Marcy galloped off with his orderly to the foot-hills on our left, to hunt for deer and elk, and we saw no more of him for several hours.

Eight miles from the Mud Volcano the trail was found, which led us over the mountains into the Madison Valley. Trail well marked, but very difficult and tiresome to follow.

At 11 o'clock we reached the summit of the great divide, and got our first glimpse of the lovely valley of the East Fork of the Madison River. The descent was extremely laborious, but we are getting now quite accustomed to almost anything.

The East Fork of the Madison meandered through the centre of the broad and level valley, and along the margin of the stream, on either side, was a luxuriant growth of willows, in places fairly covering the water. The trail crossed the Madison frequently, and great stretches of verdant meadow land, covered with wild flowers, spread out on every side.

As we were crossing the stream, several miles down the valley, a buck elk sprang from under cover of the willows and bounded off for the foot-hills. I happened to be in advance, and as my horse raised the bank the elk broke cover, something like one hundred yards away. Jumping quickly from my horse and throwing a cartridge into the barrel of my Winchester, I fired, and unquestionably missed; but the buck was running, quartering across a patch of low willows which would have nearly hidden him had he been standing. At each bound he showed his hind quarters, head and antlers, and I fired four shots in quick succession, but probably over-shot him. As the elk gained the base of the foothills, full five hundred yards from where I stood, he stopped, with head and branching antlers high in the air and flag flying as he looked back at us. His whole form was in view, and he presented a magnificent picture, one certainly that a sportsman would go into raptures over—a perfect copy of Sir Edwin Landseer's "Monarch of the Glen." My rifle was sighted for two hundred yards, and estimating the distance, I took most deliberate aim at his fore shoulder, drawing the front bead fine into the very delicate notch of my back sight; then raising the rifle quickly, two and a half feet, and covering a dark object which lay against the hill beyond and squarely over the shoulders of the animal, I pulled trigger, and I never took greater pains with a rifle-shot in all my life, and I am sure my nerves were never steadier.

I would have given everything I possessed to have cut him down handsomely at that distance. It was the first elk I had ever fired at, and right at my side, on horseback, were General Marcy and Doane, both noted hunters and famous shots. But it seems that one can never do anything well when under the influence of great anxiety.

The bullet sped along, and the elk making a bound into the willows towards the foot-hills, we saw him no more, nor could General Marcy and I find the slightest trace of him afterwards. Had he crossed the bare foot-hills towards which he was headed, we would most certainly have seen him. We beat the bushes very thoroughly for some time, as General Marcy thought he was wounded and probably hiding, but could find no blood, nor any tracks beyond the point where we last saw him. Every member of the party thought I hit him the last shot, and Doane said his tail was down when he made his last jump; but I must confess my honest judgment to be that I missed him clean at every shot. It was a great disappointment to me, although the shots were all difficult ones, in my opinion. Had the elk been running squarely across my front, instead of quartering back and nearly hidden by willows, or had he stopped at two hundred yards, instead of five hundred, so that I could have held my rifle on him, instead of over and above him, I should have killed him, without a doubt. General Marcy and I finally gave up the search—

galloped on and joined the party, which by this time was several miles in advance.

Reached the Lower Geyser Basin at 5 P. M., having accomplished twenty-six miles and the hardest day's journey yet, and we were all tired when we reached camp.

The Secretary and General Marcy stand the horseback riding over these indescribably ugly and difficult trails remarkably well. Secretary complains a little of his left leg and knee, and I believe he has suffered terribly since leaving Soda Mountain; but he is plucky, and does not make his sufferings known.

We have a lovely camp in a park of firs, affording good shade, and flowers in endless variety are growing everywhere about us. The only spring of pure water fit for drinking and cooking purposes in the whole lower basin is situated within fifty yards of our camp.

The mosquitoes are fearfully thick here, and for the first time during our trip. All of our party, except myself, brought head-nets from the Mud Volcano, but I had almost made up my mind that there were no mosquitoes or flies in this valley, and so left mine behind.

As we were leaving the depot in Chicago, General Sheridan told us we would suffer everywhere in this country from flies and mosquitoes, and advised us to go prepared to encounter them. I therefore sent to my friend Mr. George Walker to have put up for our party a preparation which our old fishing party has used for several years on the Peshtigo River—tar, oil of pennyroyal, camphor, and sweet oil. It is put up in small bottles, can be carried in one's vest pocket, and if applied to the face and hands every half hour, flies and mosquitoes will keep at a respectful distance. Pour a small quantity in the palm of one hand and rub thoroughly over face, hands, and neck. We have tried it for years in a mosquito country second to none on this continent, and it is a sure thing. Try it! Mr. Walker kindly ordered a dozen or more bottles of this mosquito medicine, had them securely packed, and sent forward from Chicago. The package caught us at Omaha, and we have carried it everywhere, and guarded it carefully. Here in the Geyser Basins we want this preparation quite as much as we want rations, but, as is usual in such cases, what we most need is left behind. Our box is at the Mud Volcano.

I had a good deal of sport this evening shooting at a target with a shingle-sight. Think I amused and mystified the gentlemen considerably. It is a good trick, and well worth describing.

Many years ago a friend of mine, John Murray, showed me the trick, and, although I have shot with the shingle in the presence of a great number of keen sportsmen, I have found but one person who fathomed the secret. George Walker, of Chicago, solved the problem. Murray went to California in 1849 and returned in 1868, having been away from his home nineteen years. He was one of the finest rifle-shots I ever knew, and a thorough sportsman. His life in California was passed largely in the mines, and he suffered the same changes of fortune that a majority of those did who followed mining solely for a livelihood—rich one day and poor the next. He told me he was "dead broke" hundreds of times, but with his rifle and shingle-sight could always win money enough to secure a good supper and bed, and generally a little loose change besides. The trick is this:

Take a shingle, from five to six inches in width, and fit it closely and securely to the muzzle of your rifle, so that the end of the barrel comes well through, and the shingle comes up flush against the front sight. The hole for the muzzle of the rifle should be cut in the centre of the shingle, and at the butt. The exact shape of the rifle-muzzle should be first marked on the shingle with a pencil, and cut out accurately with a pocket-knife, so that when the shingle is on no daylight can be seen between it and the barrel. Then place a white patch, half an inch or an inch square, on a tree at forty or fifty steps. With the shingle on the rifle I can hit the patch just as often as I can with it off, but those whom I shoot against can neither see the patch nor the tree upon which the patch or target is pinned. The front and back sights are between the eye and the shingle, but, unfortunately, the shingle hides everything in front of it. Generally, in doing this, I offer to shoot a given number of shots at a struck centre with shingle-sight, against some one using the ordinary open sights. If I chance to compete with some one who is a better rifle-shot than I am, then I lose; otherwise I win.

I will merely state that there is no guesswork about it, but that I can draw the sights finely and accurately on to the whitened head of a ten-penny nail at twenty-five yards. The party are anxious to know how the trick is done, but it will keep for a few days, and may serve to amuse us and kill time at some other point further on.

There are some fifty geysers and mud volcanoes in the Lower Basin, where we are now encamped, and we purpose looking at these things in the morning, then pass on to the more remarkable sights contained in the Upper Basin.

The day has been unusually warm, but the nights in this

valley are always so cold that blankets are in demand. In July and August the thermometer occasionally falls from ten to fifteen degrees below freezing point, and frost appears frequently. Doane says, "It never rains here, but look out for a snow-storm at any time."

The scene in and about our camp reminds me of our old Corps and Army Headquarters in the field during the war. I enjoy every moment of this life. There is a fascination about it that cannot be expressed in words.

Army reminiscences have been the principal theme this evening. General Sweitzer and Colonel Gillespie have given us some stray threads of unwritten history in relation to McClellan's Peninsula Campaign. General Forsyth has taken us down to the battle-field of Winchester, and whipped the enemy once more at Five Forks; and the Secretary has given us some rare and amusing sketches from the records of his old regiment, the Fifteenth Iowa, among the best of which was the history of Adjutant Pomutz, and the trials and tribulations of his mare, Mary. General Marcy has been rather quiet. He is certainly far from being well.

The Great Geyser Basins.

August 3.—Were in the saddle this morning promptly. Everything goes on like clockwork now, and there are no delays. Each man knows his place and keeps it, and knows his part and does it without a word.

Our party, with Doane as guide and instructor, spent two or three hours in examining the small geysers, hot springs, and mud volcanoes. None of the geysers in this basin play to any great height. Those we saw threw up columns varying in size from fifteen to forty feet. The mud volcanoes were the most interesting of anything we saw in the Lower Basin; pools or basins from three to fifty feet in diameter, boiling and sputtering, and forming every imaginable shape. Shell and flowers of every description and variety. The changes occurring in these volcanoes every moment, particularly in the smaller ones, were most marvelous and extraordinary. I can compare them to nothing but the changes of a kaleidoscope, lacking only the gorgeous colors. One would never tire in watching the innumerable forms of rare beauty which were created in rapid succession these boiling, seething caldrons.

The attention of Colonel Gillespie and myself was attracted by one very small volcano, not more than three feet in diameter, which seemed to outdo all the others in its exquisite combinations. We remained and watched its curious action long after the party had moved on. The color of the substance in this pool was very much like porcelain, and during the time we watched it, saw beautiful images manufactured and destroyed in countless numbers. A vast number of boiling springs are found in this basin. We looked at several of the largest and most interesting of the system, and then passed on to the extreme southeastern end of the lower basin.

There was no trail, and we had to pick our way over fallen timber and through dense thickets of pine, and up and down hills whose sides were precipitous, and where our horses would slip, slide, and stumble in a manner quite uncomfortable, and oftentimes extremely hazardous to both horse and rider. After

A "Good Trail"

several miles of this kind of traveling, and when our patience was nearly exhausted, we emerged from this labyrinth of down timber and struck the main trail, which runs due south to the Great Geyser Basin, following closely the windings of the Fire Hole River, which flowed past us to the north.

For five miles we splashed, floundered, and struggled on this trail, the like of which I never before saw and hope never to see again. At one point a sapling had been bent by the wind so that it hung directly over the main trail, a branch trail, however, leading around it. The main trail seemed the surest and safest, and Sweitzer, Doane, and Forsyth, who were ahead, so thought, and kept to it, passing under the sapling and managing to maintain their seats, although, stoop as low as they could, they came near being unhorsed. I came next, and passed under safely, but not without being scratched some. The Secretary came next to me and thought he could make it, but being a trifle stouter than those who had passed before him, he was raked and scraped to a fearful extent by the branches and body of the sapling itself. His coat was torn down the back and on the shoulders, and his pants ripped, and not only that, was badly scraped and marked all over. When General Belknap came out from under that sapling he bore no resemblance to a Minister of War. Spattered and plastered all over with mud, not here and there a spot, but well covered from head to foot, tattered and torn and in most thorough disorder, he presented a ludicrous appearance, and we all had to laugh, and the Secretary laughed as heartily as any one at his own condition.

At 10:30 o'clock we came to the lower geysers of the

Upper Basin, where the trail led over higher ground and became much firmer, and we had from this time on but little difficulty in making our way.

Reached camp at twenty minutes to eleven, and have passed the day in examining the geysers and hot springs.

The Upper Geyser Basin is about three miles in length and from one-half to three-quarters of a mile in width. The Fire Hole River flows along the eastern side of the valley, and is a beautiful stream, from sixty to seventy-five feet in breadth, running over a rocky bed, and is fordable at almost any point. The valley is hemmed in on every side by mountains, very heavily timbered, which rise up above the level of Fire Hole River from fifteen hundred to two thousand feet.

In this valley or basin is concentrated the most remarkable system of geysers and hot springs known in the world. More than one hundred active geysers and up to this date fifteen hundred hot springs have been discovered. Each geyser and each spring differ from the other in its class, style, beauty, and power. To describe them all would be an impossibility without spending weeks here. To convey in a written description the faintest idea of the grandeur of any particular one of the large geysers when in full play or the marvelous beauty of its crater and scalloped basins, which lie in terraced steps down its sloping sides and along its base, is an impossibility, at least for me. Lieutenant Doane, Professor Hayden, Captain Barlow, and Lieutenant Jones, in their reports, have come as near accurate descriptions as is possible.

I do not propose to undertake any such laborious work as would be involved in writing up for the fifth time the Great Geyser Basin. I am merely keeping a daily journal of passing

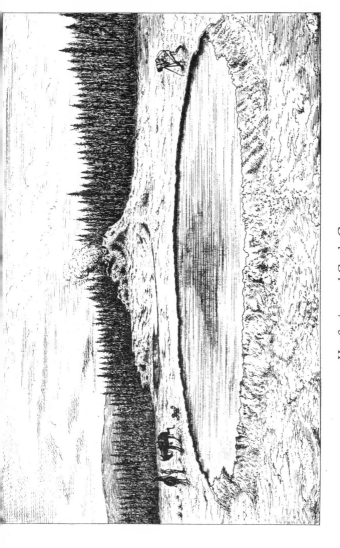

Hot Spring and Castle Geyser

events, not writing a scientific report, for that is entirely outside my province. I have not attempted and shall not attempt to give geological formations of mountains, cañons, rocks, and geysers, or the mineral properties of the hot springs. For all this information I refer to the several reports of the distinguished gentlemen who have examined this country by direction of officers high in command and the Congress of the United States. I shall give, however, my own impressions of these wonderful and mysterious things, and brief descriptions of a few of the large geysers.

At the head of the Basin, and the last one in the group, stands Old Faithful, just one-quarter of a mile from our camp and facing us. Next in order, and a few hundred yards further north and on the east side of Fire Hole River, stand The Bee-Hive, Giantess, and Steamboat group. On the west side of river and to the north of us stands the Castle. On the east side and nearly opposite the Castle stands the Grand. On the northwest side the Giant and the Grotto, and on the northeast side of the river are the Riverside and Fan group.

The first five in rank among the geysers named above are Giantess, Grand, Giant, Old Faithful, and Bee-Hive.

Old Faithful plays hourly, day and night, throwing a column of water three by seven feet to the height of one hundred and fifty feet.

The Bee-Hive plays irregularly, but can be counted upon with certainty once during every twenty-four hours, and ejects a column twenty-six inches in diameter to the height of two hundred and twenty-six feet.

The Giantess has no regular periods of eruption, but usually plays once during every forty-eight hours, and throws a column twenty-three feet in diameter to the height of ninety to one hundred feet. There are also five jets that radiate from the main column of water, and some of these reach a height of two hundred feet.

The Steamboat group is composed of four geysers, which erupt very irregularly, seldom reaching one hundred feet in height, the columns varying in size from one to three feet in diameter. Lieutenant Doane has seen two of this group play.

The Castle plays several times each day, rarely giving its maximum eruption, but generally throws a column two feet in diameter to the height of sixty feet.

The Grand plays to the greatest height of any, and discharges a column three feet in diameter to the height of three hundred feet, but its periods are very irregular. Doane has been in this basin four times, and has never yet seen it in action. Professor Hayden's party and also Captain Barlow's party saw it in full play.

The Giant ejects a column seven feet in diameter to a height of from ninety to two hundred feet, and is usually seen once in every twenty-four hours.

The Grotto group plays irregularly three or four times in every twenty-four hours, and throws a column to the height of fifty or sixty feet, but in separate jets through different apertures in the crater.

The Riverside plays irregularly, and is rarely seen—throws a small column about eight inches in diameter to the height of fifty or sixty feet.

The Fan group is composed of three geysers in fan shape, which throw columns about eight inches in diameter to the height of fifty or sixty feet, the jets crossing each other and giving a very beautiful appearance. They play several times each day, but at no regular periods. Its eruptions produce a loud, rushing noise, with water and steam alternately. The water issuing from all the geysers varies from one hundred and ninety-eight to two hundred and twelve degrees of heat, and is impregnated with silica and lime.

In addition to the above there are from eighty to ninety other geysers, which throw small columns of water from ten to forty feet in height.

We have seen the following large geysers play to-day: Grand, Grotto, Bee-Hive, Castle, and Fan Group.

This evening the wind was from the north, and carried the column of water and steam from Old Faithful to the south, while we stood within thirty feet of it when in full play. It was the grandest spectacle I ever beheld. A great caldron, extending into the very bowels of the earth, for aught we know, and heated by unknown fires, bubbling, boiling, and every sixty minutes emitting a column of water, three by seven feet, to the height of one hundred and fifty feet. Just before the eruption takes place the roaring, hissing, and rumbling of this mass of boiling water is fearful. Finally the water begins boiling over the rim of the basin, or mouth of the crater, and jet follows jet in quick succession, each convulsion sending the water higher, until the column reaches its greatest height. The immense clouds of steam which float above and around this great mass of boiling water makes the column appear three or four times its actual size. The column remains at its maximum height from five to seven minutes. Of course the quantity of water ejected at each eruption is enormous.

When the sun strikes these playing columns of water at

the proper angle the scene is perfectly gorgeous. At 6 this evening we were all standing near Old Faithful while playing. The sun was low, just touching the western range of mountains which shuts in, in that direction, this valley of wonders. The column was one grand mass of gorgeous colors. Three rainbows were seen extending across the playing column, and the falling spray seemed like countless millions of diamonds and precious gems. The hissing and roaring of the boiling water; the rushing of the overflow as it poured down the terraced slopes of the crater; the rainbows and falling spray, so beautifully colored and tinted; the mass of steam and vapor floating off towards the mountain range in the east and south; the smooth lawn in the background and to the north, carpeted with fresh grass and decked with flowers, where our white tents were pitched, and where horses and mules were grazing; the majestic mountain ranges which hemmed us in on the east, west, and south, thickly wooded from base to peak with pine and spruce, the dark green forming a rich contrast with the more striking colors of the playing column; and beyond our tents and camp; and down the basin to the north, and along the Fire-Hole River on both sides for two and a half miles, puffing jets and long, steady columns of steam and vapor rising from a hundred geysers and a thousand springs, looking for all the world like a fleet of Mississippi River steamboats stemming a swift current and working slowly up to join us. All this within our sight was so very grand and beautiful that none of us can ever forget it.

The view at the summit of the Rocky Mountains, where we saw the stream divide—the waters of one flowing to the Pacific and of the other to the Atlantic; the charming scenery of Port Neuf and Ryan's Cañons; the grandeur of Washburn and the panoramic view from its summit of snow-capped peaks, broad valleys and lakes, and flowers growing luxuriantly by banks of snow and frozen brooks; the Grand Cañon of the Yellowstone and the Great Falls, three hundred and fifty feet at a single bound; the wild mountain scenery that has been spread out before us all along our trail from Ellis; indeed, everything we have seen thus far on this trip sinks into utter insignificance by comparison with the Grand Geysers and Boiling Springs of the Upper Basin of the Yellowstone Park. It is no easy undertaking to get here. A person must be in perfect health and strength to endure the horseback-ride over this mountain trail. I have seen some campaigning over what was called a rough country, but I must confess that I had no conception of what was involved in two hundred and fifty miles on horseback with a pack-train over the Yellowstone trail. Those weary miles, through dense thickets and over fallen timber, with trunks and limbs entwined and interlaced, and where one's eyes grow tired in looking for open spaces to crowd through; those miles of narrow trail up and down steep mountains and along the sides of cañons, where chasms yawn hundreds of feet beneath you, and where one misstep of your horse would send you to sure destruction, all have to be retraced on our return. But if it were ten times as long and ten times as difficult and dangerous, one sight of Old Faithful in full play, as we witnessed it to-night, and one view of this valley to the north, as I can see it now, would amply repay any one for all the difficulties to be encountered.

The Boiling Springs vary in size and shape. There are over fifteen hundred in all and no two exactly alike, although a majority of their basins are round, and as perfect in shape as a sculptor could make with mallet and chisel. Some are boiling and running over, others are quiet, and a person would hardly believe the water was hot enough to burn without testing it. The water in all the pools is of the deepest blue. I never saw such tints, and so clear that one can see to the depth of thirty feet and trace the exquisite linings of the basins as accurately as in the shallow pools, which lie in almost endless numbers outside and down the sloping surface. The wonderful beauty of the incrustations upon the sides and bottoms of these fairy caverns is indescribable. The general appearance of these linings is that of cliffs and beds of coral, but worked up in fantastic forms of surpassing beauty.

The little basins which lie outside the larger ones are, perhaps, the most exquisitely beautiful. There are hundreds— thousands, sometimes—at the base of a single spring, some of them gorgeously colored and tinted, and the delicate and intricate tracery of the inner coatings, formed by the action of the water flowing in unceasingly and keeping the surface disturbed, is wonderful.

The description I have written of the geysers and springs in this basin is brief and tame, and falls so far short of the reality, that I refer the reader to Doane's report and his graphic account of this valley and its wonders, as he saw it in 1870.

The pack-train made eight miles to-day, and we traveled sixteen.

The Secretary, Forsyth, and myself had a bath about 4 o'clock P. M. in the Fire Hole River, and were much refreshed.

General Marcy is quite ill to-night, and the Doctor insists upon his keeping very quiet. His bath in the Yellowstone day before yesterday, and going several hours without changing his wet clothes, is undoubtedly the cause. The General is the most remarkable man for one of his years I have ever met. We all think him very imprudent. Has hunted very hard, sometimes riding miles away from the trail, working almost indefatigably, early and late, to kill an elk or deer; but this is the most barren country for game at this season of the year I have ever seen, and nothing has been killed by the party but grouse, with which our table has been well supplied. General Marcy thinks he can ride as fast and far and hunt as hard as he could thirty-five years ago, but I doubt if he can. "Quien sabe?" says he.

We now hope to break camp in the morning, and move about eighteen miles on our return trip, which will bring us to the spot where I shot at the elk, near the crossing on the East Fork of the Madison. Hope to see more of the large geysers play before we leave. The day has been warm, and the mosquitoes have annoyed us exceedingly.

August 4.—General Marcy was very, very ill last night, and this morning we were all alarmed at his condition. Had congestive chills, and the Doctor and General Belknap were up with him greater portion of the night.

We remain here to-day, as it would be neither safe nor prudent for General Marcy to undertake the journey. If he keeps quiet to-day we hope he may be able to travel a short distance tomorrow, but unless he improves materially we may have to remain here several days. Our riding horses are pretty thoroughly used up, and several of the pack-mules, whose saddles do not fit, have sore backs. A few days' rest would do the animals good, but we would have to live on short rations, as we only brought five days' supplies, and this is the third day out. The water from the Fire Hole River, which we are forced to drink, is bad, and Doane tells us it is not safe to use it for more than two or three days. The water from the geysers and hot springs flows into it the whole length of the valley. The day has been cool and delightful, a strong breeze blowing from the northeast.

This morning, immediately after breakfast, I took my rifle and hunted for several miles along the base of the mountain range to the west of the basin, hoping to kill a grouse for the General, but the only game I saw on my long tramp was one red squirrel, which I was fortunate enough to kill, and which the cook made into soup that Marcy seemed to relish. The party have been lying about camp most of the day, getting thoroughly rested and in condition for the return trip.

Old Faithful has continued her grand exhibitions promptly at the beginning of each hour, but the other geysers have been unusually quiet. At 6 o'clock, and while we were at dinner, the Bee Hive gave us a fine display. Our camp is pitched on the west side of the river and directly opposite this geyser. We rushed quickly to the river bank, and remained until the eruption ceased. The column was two hundred and twenty-six feet in height and twenty-six inches in diameter, and remained at its maximum height for the space of fifteen minutes by the watch. The sun struggled through the clouds about this time, and as the sunlight struck the playing geyser, from a point just above the wooded summit of the western mountain range, the whole column of boiling water, steam, and spray was a mass of gorgeous color. This is the second time we have seen this geyser in action.

A few minutes before 7 o'clock the Secretary, Colonel Gillespie, and myself walked up the valley to Old Faithful and got to it just in time to see the first jets shoot up, and at the same time the Castle broke out, below our camp, followed quickly by the Grotto group, further down, and we had a fine view of the three geysers playing simultaneously. Doane was in camp, and said the display made by the Castle was the finest he has yet seen.

Instead of snow, as was predicted, we were treated to a thunder shower this afternoon. It was of brief duration, however, and when the clouds broke and the sun came out, a double rainbow appeared, extending from the southwest to the southeast. It was, like everything else we see in the Geyser Basin, grander and more beautiful than any rainbow we ever looked at. The upper bow seemed twelve feet in width, and extended from horizon to horizon, six feet of its upper margin being the richest crimson, the next three feet of purple, and the lower margin the deepest blue. It lasted for some time, and we all watched it until it faded and disappeared.

If General Marcy is well enough in the morning we shall move, if we only make half a dozen miles. We must make a desperate effort to get him out of this basin to some point where he can have pure water. He will certainly die if compelled to stay here. The Secretary is troubled and alarmed at his condition to-night, and Dr. Whitefoot is very anxious. It would be terrible for General Marcy to be seriously ill here. If we could only get him to Ellis, where he could be properly nursed and get suitable food and medicines, I have no doubt he would get along, for he has a strong will and an iron constitution in his favor. I think the General is alarmed himself and fears he is going to be dangerously ill, although he says but little about it.

August 5.—Two English gentlemen who have been spending some days in this basin told us that the Grand Geyser had played for the three nights preceding last night between 8 and 9 o'clock. We accordingly watched for it to-night, but were disappointed in our expectations. It was convulsed five times at intervals of fifteen minutes, and threw up great jets as high as fifteen or sixteen feet, but that was all, and at 10 o'clock we gave up all hopes of seeing it play, and returned to camp.

General Marcy had a bad night and is no better this morning. Had a high fever after midnight, and complains of soreness in his bowels. We have been at a loss to know what to do. Have but one day's provisions after to-day, and if the General is not able to be moved, the situation will be precarious indeed. He is certainly not able to ride on horseback, but one thing is certain, he must be moved out of this basin where better water can be had. After consultation, it was decided that Doane should construct a litter, to be carried by two pack-mules; and if General Marcy can be induced to try it, we might get him out, at least as far as our last camp, where there is a spring of clear, cold water. General Forsyth has despatched three of the best men to Yellowstone Lake to bring up our entire outfit as quickly as possible. Doane has just completed his litter, and I will attempt to describe it:

Two poles, eighteen feet long and four inches in diameter, were lashed together in the centre, for the distance of seven feet, by weaving a network of pack-cord across and forming a good, strong bed of sufficient width to admit a mule between the poles in front and one behind. The mules are to be fastened to this litter in precisely the same manner that a horse would be attached to the shafts of a buggy, the shafts of the litter being strongly fastened to pack-saddles by means of straps. Upon the bed of the litter a buffalo robe was spread, and upon this a mattress was placed, with plenty of blankets and a pillow. Two of the most gentle and surest footed mules were selected and hitched in, with a reliable man on the back of each.

General Marcy watched from his tent the construction of this litter, which, I think, he describes minutely in one of his own books, "The Prairie Traveler," but said nothing. When it was finished the Secretary asked him how he liked the looks of it, and said further that he would be pleased to have him try it. General Marcy consented to the arrangement without a word, and we soon had him on the litter and made as comfortable as possible. There is no doubt about the litter being splendid for the open country and a level trail, but how it will work over the trail which we are forced to follow remains to be seen.

One of the non-commissioned officers, in charge of a party with axes, was sent out early to construct a new trail along the base of the foot-hills, to avoid the terrible swamp which we crossed coming from the Lower Basin. This party has just returned, and reports having cut out a new road which we can follow with but little difficulty. Our camp is now being struck, and we shall be off in a few minutes.

We left our camp in the Grand Geyser Basin at 9:30 o'clock this morning and marched fifteen miles, going into camp at 2 P.M. on the North Fork of the Madison, about two miles to the west of Elk Crossing. It has been a good day for moving our patient, as the sun has been obscured by clouds and rain has fallen lightly at intervals. Doane's litter has proved a great success, and Marcy has stood the ride of fifteen miles much better than we anticipated and seems more comfortable to-night. We believe now he is going to get along. It was a good thing bringing him out of the Geyser Basin, as he would certainly have died had he remained there any length of time. In crossing the great marsh, near our camp at the Lower Basin, the rear mule of the litter mired badly at one point and after struggling fiercely went down, throwing the General out. He was sleeping at the time, and was not a little astonished to find himself thus unceremoniously dumped from his bed. He received no injury, but was well covered with mud. Our journey to-morrow will be much more tiresome for Marcy, as we have to cross the Great Divide; and how the litter is to be carried by mules up that narrow, precipitous, and tortuous trail and over the masses of fallen timber is a problem to me. Doane says it can be done, but I am a little doubtful.

We crossed the Fire Hole River near the upper end of the Lower Basin, and saw the Great Hot Spring group, the largest one of which is four hundred and fifty yards in circumference. It is the largest spring yet discovered in this country.

We have a fine camp in a grassy bottom near the river, and good grazing for the stock. The party is in good spirits this evening at the marked improvement in General Marcy.

August 6.—Last night was damp and cold, and a thick coating of ice formed in the water-buckets which were outside our tents. When we ate breakfast the ground was white with frost. I started out in advance of the party with my orderly, in hope of killing a deer, and traveled along the foot-hills, hunting the valley to the south of the Madison thoroughly, but saw no game or fresh signs. Just before reaching the base of the Divide, I killed a mountain grouse and a red squirrel, so Marcy will have something palatable for his supper.

We were an hour going up the Divide, reaching its summit at 11:30. The ascent was not as difficult as the descent. Marcy rode in the litter part of the way, but finally the trail became so steep and the timber so thick that he was compelled to take to his horse and ride the last few hundred yards. The litter was taken apart, carried up by the men, and put together again at the summit. At 12 M. we were again in motion, and at 3:30 P.M. reached our old camping-ground at the Mud Volcano. General Marcy came in one hour behind us, having slept most of the time after leaving the summit, and was feeling quite fresh and bright, and the Doctor is confident he will continue to improve.

The men who left camp yesterday morning to bring up the supplies from Yellowstone Lake saw four grizzlies while passing over the Divide, and after a sharp fight killed one of them.

We found the fishing here just as fine as before, and caught magnificent strings. Forsyth used my light Orvis rod, and although he had great success in striking the fish, it took time and careful management to land them with such light, delicate tackle and in such rapid water. Nearly half the men were fishing with short, stiff rods and strong cords, and all had extraordinary luck, so that the pile of trout brought into camp was enormous.

After dinner, and while we were sitting about the campfire, a band of elk was seen a few hundred yards from us, running

87

about among our animals, which were grazing in the river bottom. Doane and I sprang for our rifles, but failed in getting a shot.

The programme for to-morrow is to leave our camp here, take our lunch baskets, and go on horseback to Yellowstone Lake, where we propose spending the day, returning in the evening with the remainder of our camp equipage and supplies; and we anticipate much pleasure.

August 7.—Breakfast at 8 o'clock, and started soon after for Yellowstone Lake, distant six miles.

The trail led us along the river, across narrow valleys bright with rich verdure and brilliant with wild flowers, through which invariably ran dashing mountain streams. Frequently through vistas in the forest we caught glimpses of a high, snow-capped mountain range in the east. Wherever we touched the banks of the Yellowstone great numbers of trout were seen of enormous size, swimming in water which was so clear that every motion of the fish could be distinctly seen, and we were tempted several times to stop, but thought it best to postpone fishing until our return trip in the evening.

As we neared the Lake we came out of the rough, hilly country into a broad stretch of meadow-land, smooth as a billiard table, with clusters of pine and willow along the margin of the river and many little lakes scattered about, with here and there a bayou or lagoon cutting into the Yellowstone.

From the river, lakes, and bayous great flocks of wild fowl arose, among which we saw geese, brant, swan, pelican, and sand-hill cranes, blue herons, and a large variety of ducks, including the mallard, red-head, green and blue-winged teal, widgeon, and pintails. I fired at a flock of wild geese three hundred yards distant, and at the report of the rifle large numbers of wild fowl got up all about us from lakes and streams which were before hidden from our view.

When within a mile of the Lake we came to a spur of considerable height, shooting squarely across our route from river to mountain range. When we reached the highest point another scene of unequalled beauty burst upon us without the slightest warning. There at our very feet lay Yellowstone Lake in all its grandeur, shut in by mountains of great altitude, their summits and sides white with perpetual snow. To the south and a little to the west loomed up Mount Sheridan, the loftiest, grandest, and whitest peak of all, towering thirteen thousand feet above the sea; and adjoining Sheridan and completing the circle were Mount Stevenson, Mount Humphreys, Mount Sangford, Mount Doane, and others of almost equal size and grandeur, but nameless as yet. Yonder, and almost within sight, among the snowy cliffs, rise the Yellowstone, the Big Horn, the Madison, and the Gallatin, four of the principal tributaries of the Missouri, all flowing to the north eventually after a run of nearly four thousand miles, finding the Atlantic Ocean at the mouth of the Mississippi; and in the same belt of Snow Mountains, the Snake River begins, fed by the same springs and the same banks of snow as the Yellowstone, but trends in a westerly course hundreds of miles before it mingles its water with those of the Columbia, en route to the Pacific Ocean. Green River, the main tributary of the Colorado, also rises among the mountain peaks in sight, and after weary windings in the dark cañons of the Colorado, reaches the Pacific through the Gulf of California.

Yellowstone Lake, by Doane's measurement, lies seven

thousand seven hundred and fourteen and three-fifths feet above the sea [actually it is 7,733 feet high—R.A.B.], and with the exception only of Lake Titicaca, on the head waters of the Madeira River in Peru, is the highest great body of water known, its waters being one thousand four hundred and twenty-nine feet above the highest summit of Mount Washington, while all around it majestic mountains loom up from five to six thousand feet above its level.

Yellowstone Lake is triangular in shape, and measures twenty-six miles from northwest to southeast, between the points where the river flows in and where it flows out. From the foot of the Lake, where the river leaves it, to its extreme southwestern limit, is thirty-three miles. Its greatest width is eighteen miles and greatest known depth fifty fathoms. Along its eastern shore numerous tributaries enter from the eastern range bordering it. On the south shore of the Lake sharp spurs stand out boldly to the water's edge, forming bays and channels between. It is one hundred and fifty miles around the Lake, following the shore line, and the Lake itself, according to Captain Barlow, contains an area of fourteen hundred square miles. There are a dozen or more islands in the Lake, containing an area of from fifty to six hundred acres. These islands are generally flat and thickly timbered, and many are rocky, but none mountainous.

We moved down to the Lake about 10:30 o'clock, and halted at our camp, which had been established August 1st. Found our large tent pitched in a grove of pine on the bank of the Lake, with an open grassy meadow in the rear, and directly opposite our camp is Stevenson's Island, the only one that has been named to this date.

Lunch at Yellowstone Lake

Six miles south from Stevenson's Island, and eight miles south from our camp, lies the largest island in the Lake, containing an area of six hundred acres. It is heavily timbered, has many springs of pure water, and fine meadows. We named this "Belknap Island," in honor of the Secretary of War.

We lay in the shade of the pines for several hours, enjoying the strong breeze from the south and the grand view of Lake and snow-capped mountains, waiting patiently for the return of the only sail-boat. One Commodore Topping has established himself on the banks of the Yellowstone in a log hut, and has a fine boat for the use of tourists. As we came in sight of the Lake this morning the boat was well out and heading for Pelican Creek, with Lieutenants Green and Quinton, who came in last night from Ellis, by the way of Baronette's, on the eastern side of the Yellowstone. We have been firing rifles and pistols to attract the attention of the party and to get it to return with the boat but it was 12:30 P.M. when we discovered the boat returning. At 1:30 P.M. the party arrived at our camp and lunched with us. Baronette came down with the officers referred to, expecting to take General Marcy and myself back over same route for a three days' hunt, as talked of the evening we reached Tower Falls, but owing to the illness of Marcy and lack of time, we have concluded to give up the hunt. General Marcy and I have had great expectations in regard to this expedition with Baronette, and it is a great disappointment to me to abandon it, as I shall probably never again have such an opportunity.

Lieutenants Green and Quinton, Baronette, and Sergeant Anderson killed on the trip a grizzly, an elk, and six deer, and they saw a great many more, while on this side of the river we have seen very few.

Baronette will join our party to-morrow night at the foot of Mount Washburn, and we are to have a day's hunting high up the mountains, where Baronette thinks he can show me a grizzly.

We spent the day about the Lake, enjoying every moment, but the wind was too strong and the sea too heavy to take a sail, as we had intended.

Left for the Mud Volcano at 5 o'clock, and when within a mile and a half of camp we halted, got out our fishing tackle, and tried once more to catch trout with flies. They were rising by hundreds everywhere in the river. It was useless, however. I caught one, but no more were taken. The Secretary and most of the party rode on to camp, while General Forsyth, Captain Hossack, and myself remained with our orderlies, and after satisfying ourselves that fly-fishing was a useless waste of time, commenced baiting with grasshoppers and had capital sport. In one hour and five minutes Forsyth and I caught thirty trout of immense size. I do not know the weight of the string, but it was all one could do to lift it clear from the ground. We reached camp before dark and found General Marcy improving steadily, so that in a couple of days, we think, he will be able to ride his horse and give up the litter.

Homeward Bound.

August 8.—Broke camp at 7 o'clock and moved towards Ellis. Last night was one of the coldest we have experienced on the trip. A heavy frost covered the ground this morning, and the water froze three-fourths of an inch in buckets during the night. For the first hour of our march we were all uncomfortably cold, but in the middle of the day the sun became very hot.

The white mule gave us such an extra performance this morning that it took all the packers to hold him while he was packed, giving unmistakable evidence of not yet being subdued. The rascal, notwithstanding his antics, has afforded great amusement for the party during the entire journey.

We traveled over the old trail until we came within two miles of the Upper Falls, when we bore off to the east, following the Yellowstone River and crossing Cascade Creek near its mouth. Went into camp about noon, at the foot of Washburn, having made twenty miles. Our tents are pitched in a balsam grove, nine thousand feet above the sea and two thousand feet below the summit of Washburn. Wild flowers are growing about our camp in great variety, and many of them surpass in rich color any we have before seen. Flowers seem to grow everywhere in this country; in groves of pine, spruce, and balsam, where they seldom get a ray of sunshine; in dense thickets, where a straggling sunbeam rarely enters; on every open stretch of meadow-land, and from out the rocky crevices of the highest ranges, where no soil can be seen, they appear to grow as luxuriantly and with as much color as in the valleys or on the sloping hillsides. General Belknap gathered this evening, within fifty feet of his tent, twenty-three varieties, and has pressed them between the leaves of a book to take home.

From a ridge just below our camp we have an excellent view of the Yellowstone Basin, which we are now rapidly leaving behind. The first hour's march over the trail to-morrow will shut it out completely, and possibly forever, so far as any member of this party is concerned.

Baronette joined us about 5 p.m., and we will take our hunt to-morrow. Starting at daylight, we will pass along the summit of the great snowy range that lies to the west and north of Washburn.

The remainder of the party will follow the main trail over the western slope of Washburn, and camp to-morrow night at Baronette's cabin, on the east fork of the Yellowstone, where we expect to join them about dark, having over forty miles to make by the route Baronette has indicated; and it will undoubtedly be a hard day on us.

General Marcy told Baronette this evening that if he was fortunate enough to encounter a grizzly, he must give me a chance, which he has promised to do, but I may not care to improve any chance of this sort when the time comes.

A Day in the Mountains with Baronette.

August 9.—We were a little late in getting started this morning, but were finally off, rifle in hand, at a quarter before five, and reached the summit of the great range, just west from Washburn, at 5:30 A.M. Found the ascent difficult, dangerous, and tiresome in the extreme, but rode our horses all the way up. Baronette took the lead, and I followed his trail as closely as I could, with my orderly, stopping every few minutes to let our horses breathe, then pushing on again. We wound backwards and forwards, describing great circles on the mountain's side, but all the time working slowly up towards a snowy peak which Baronette had pointed out soon after leaving camp.

Leaving the Mud Volcano
7 A.M., August 8, 1875

The scene that burst upon us as we gained this peak, ten thousand five hundred feet above the sea, and nearly on a level with Mount Washburn, was magnificent. At our feet, two thousand feet below, lay our camp, the white tents nestling closely among the balsams, while the smoke from the fires curled gracefully above the treetops, and floated gently off to the westward. Back of the camp, on a smooth grassy lawn, the horses and mules were quietly grazing, and a little further to the west the men could be seen stirring about the camp preparing their breakfast. To the south lay, spread out in all its marvelous beauty and grandeur, the Great Valley of the Yellowstone. Language utterly fails to convey the faintest description of this early morning picture as we saw it.

Yellowstone Lake, with its snowy background, the water looking bluer than ever; the river winding its way towards the Great Falls and Cañon, now and then affording a glimpse of it as it rounded the base of some gigantic mountain, or came sweeping grandly through the intervening valleys, now smooth and placid, then dashing swiftly over rocks and bowlders, and forming cascades of wonderful beauty. Nearer to us, the Great Falls of the Yellowstone were visible from where we stood, and below and nearer still, the Grand Cañon, with one hundred and fifty feet of its eastern face in plain view; also the Upper and Lower Geyser Basins, with their ten thousand jets of vapor and steam, rising from geyser and spring, and floating over the entire valley; the Sulphur Springs, the Mud Volcano, the Three Sisters, the Devil's Caldron, the Great Divide between the East Fork of the Madison and Yellowstone Rivers, over which we have but recently brought General Marcy in Doane's famous litter—

all this was in sight, and although many miles distant, seemed but a stone's throw from where we stood.

Around us mountains of every conceivable shape, with all the rounded outlines and jagged angles incident to such scenery; bays and sheltered nooks of green running high up on the mountain's side until they were lost in snow-banks or in forests of pine; great gorges cutting into the summits of the highest ranges, where the snow lies many feet in depth all the year round; vales and chasms; bald knobs, dotted on their slopes with black, stunted pines. The grandeur, sublimity, and solitude of this scene was almost oppressive.

While we stood gazing at it, the sun came peeping over the eastern range, lighting up mountain, valley, lake, river, and wooded slopes; and the clouds of vapor and steam from geysers and springs, and the mist which hung in a heavy mass over the Great Falls of the Yellowstone were exquisitely shaded and tinted by the sunlight as it spread out and covered the face of this Valley of Wonders. We checked our horses and let them rest for some minutes, while I enjoyed this last look at the mysterious country, with the air so keen that I fairly shivered.

At 6 o'clock we mounted our horses again, turned to the westward, and began our hunt. Our route was here pointed out by Baronette. A great range of mountains stretched out to the west and north, and twenty-five miles from us loomed up an immense bald peak, wooded heavily at its base, which was eight miles from Baronette's cabin. The range was in the form of a bow, and lies between Gardiner's River and Tower River. This mountain range, which seemed to be continuous, was not so, as every few miles we came to an immense gorge, or "bite," as Baronette called it, but which was, in reality, a cañon, with a swift mountain stream flowing at the bottom, and with sides precipitous and heavily timbered. Gaining the summits of mountain peaks, where the snow lies in heavy masses all the year round, is easy work compared with crossing the deep gorges which cut into these mountain ranges at regular intervals. The trees have been falling here for centuries, and such a network of limbs, trunks, and stumps has been formed, that to face it with a horse and attempt a passage is enough to appall the stoutest heart. Professor Hayden, Doane, Barlow, and Jones, all speak of making their way at different times through these labyrinths, and from four to five miles was thought to be a good day's work for a pack-train with a well-equipped pioneer corps. We struck and passed five or six of these gorges during the day.

The summit of the range was very beautiful, and generally quite easy to travel over on horseback. What appeared from the valleys to be sharp peaks and narrow ridges, when reached, were found in many cases to be level prairies, covered with grass and flowers. Little basins were found, of from two to four acres in size, with lakes of the purest, coldest water; snow-banks here and there, and flowers of the rarest, richest colors lining the slopes and growing close up to the snow. On the very summit of one of the highest peaks which we crossed to-day, and on the grassy slopes of a basin containing a lake such as I have described, where the snow lay around its margin to the depth of six or eight feet, I counted from my horse thirty varieties of wild flowers, and many of them within six inches of the snow margin or rim of the lake. The flowers grew in such profusion here that at every step the rarest blossoms were crushed. I could have lingered all day about some of those lovely spots.

We hunted cautiously along the summit of the mountain, dismounting and leading our horses, with rifles in hand, whenever fresh signs of game were observed. The fresh tracks of grizzlies were plenty, but those of mountain sheep and elk were scarce. We started one large bear and followed him up closely for some time; but he got into a thick mass of fallen timber, where it was impossible to follow on horseback, and Baronette would not go in after him on foot nor permit me to do so. The hunters in this country have no hesitation in attacking a grizzly or cinnamon bear on horseback single-handed, but very few of them will fire a shot when dismounted; the danger is too great.

At 11:30 o'clock, and while we were passing along a narrow ridge of one of the highest peaks and approaching a cañon, I happened to turn my head towards Baronette, who was slightly in rear, and I saw him off his horse with his rifle to his shoulder. Looking quickly in the direction towards which the rifle was pointed, I saw the antlers of three deer rising clear above the rocky edge of the gorge on our front. They were standing on a shelf of rock a few feet below the level of the range, and directly on the side or face of the gorge, their bodies entirely hidden, and only a portion of the neck of the one standing nearest exposed. I sprang from my horse and threw up my rifle, expecting every instant to hear the crack of Baronette's gun. As the rifle came to my face and my eye glanced down the sights, not more than four or six inches of the deer's neck could be seen. At this I fired, and no cleaner, handsomer shot was ever made. The bullet went straight to the centre of the target, and with a wild bound high into the air the buck went rolling and tumbling down the precipice with a broken neck. I ran quickly to the brink of the chasm, loading my rifle as I ran, hoping to get a shot at one of the others; but the distance was so short from the shelf where the game was standing to the thick timber that the remaining deer were in it and out of sight before I could get up. The buck I had fired at lay stone dead in a ravine fifty or seventy-five feet down the gorge. I paced the distance from where I fired to the brink of the gorge, and it was one hundred good steps. The shelf upon which the deer were standing was ten steps further, making the total distance one hundred and ten yards.

I asked Baronette why he did not fire, and he replied that he was waiting to give me the shot. I was wicked enough, however, to think for a few minutes that he did not care to risk his reputation as a rifle shot by firing at six inches of a deer's neck at such a distance; but upon reflection I am satisfied he waited for me to shoot first, fulfilling sacredly the promise he made to General Marcy last night, that if game was seen I should have the first shot.

Had I missed the deer Baronette could not have hit it, as the first jump would have been off the shelf into the thick timber of the cañon below. Baronette complimented me very highly upon the shot, saying he had never seen a finer one made at a deer. It proved to be a magnificent black-tailed buck, with horns in the velvet. Baronette at first thought it would not be possible to pack the whole deer into camp, on account of the very rough country we had to travel over, but finally concluded to try it, and in a few minutes the deer was properly dressed, and the three of us were able to elevate the carcass on to the pack-saddle of an extra horse brought along by Baronette, and we soon had him strapped and bound on with pack-cords. The point where the deer was killed was twenty miles from Baronette's cabin, over the roughest and most difficult part of the day's journey. In crossing the cañons and crowding through the down timber and dense undergrowth the deer got loose from the pack, and we had to stop several times to rearrange the cords.

About 5 o'clock we came to the great bald mountain pointed out in the morning. As we reached the top Baronette conducted me to a rocky point where a number of bowlders of large size were piled up, and said, "Here is where I found Mr. Everts after fifteen days' search." We dismounted here and rested for a few moments, while Baronette gave me the story, which was substantially as follows:

Mr. Everts was a Government official, stationed at Helena or Virginia City, and accompanied General Washburn and Lieutenant Doane on the first expedition made in 1870. On the 9th of September he got separated in some way from the party near Yellow Mountain, southwest from Yellowstone Lake, and as he did not return to camp in the evening Doane fired signal guns and kept watch-fires burning on high points during the night, but without success. For four or five days the party searched faithfully for the missing man, but at length gave him up, supposing him to be lost beyond the faintest hope of recovery. The friends and relatives of Mr. Everts, in Montana and elsewhere, joined in offering a large reward for his recovery; and Baronette, who was known to be the most skillful mountaineer in the country, was earnestly requested to undertake the search, which he did; and at the close of the fifteenth day, while skirting the base of an adjoining mountain, he saw on the summit of the bald peak before referred to something crawling on the ground among the rocks, which he at first took for a young bear. He approached cautiously, rifle in hand, and it was not until he came very near that he discovered it to be a human being, with clothing nearly stripped and worn from his person, which was reduced to skin and bones; hair long, and matted with dirt; eyesight nearly gone; unable to speak; and crawling on hands and feet among the rocks, looking for grasshoppers and bugs for food. He had been lost for thirty-seven days, and probably another day or two would have ended his sufferings. Baronette made a camp upon the spot and at once sent a man who was with him (Prichette) to Fort Ellis for an ambulance and a surgeon. For two days Baronette nursed Everts tenderly, at the end of which time he was sufficiently recovered in strength to be moved twenty miles down the trail to the cabin of some miners, who were prospecting for gold, and within ten days or two weeks was able to be sent forward to Bozeman.

We reached camp, near Baronette's cabin, at 7:30 o'clock, while our party was at dinner. We brought in the deer, but it was scraped and marred considerably by coming in contact with the limbs and trunks of trees which we encountered. We made during the day at least forty miles—the most laborious day's sport I ever had. I shall, however, long remember it with pleasure.

General Marcy abandoned his litter at the last camp, mounted his horse, and hunted faithfully during the forenoon, keeping well away from the trail, but saw nothing.

The party have had superb fishing this afternoon in the

East Fork of the Yellowstone, taking one hundred and fifty or more large trout, of which Forsyth bagged thirty, the largest string brought in; although Marcy, Gillespie, and the Secretary were quite successful.

August 10.—Broke camp at 7 o'clock and moved down to Baronette's cabin, where we stopped for an hour examining the curious and beautiful specimens of fossils, minerals, &c., he has collected from the Wind River range of mountains, Specimen Mountain, and from the entire Valley of the Yellowstone. After purchasing some of these we moved on, reached Soda Mountain at 1 P.M. encamping on our old ground.

About 4 o'clock the Sergeant in charge of pack-train reported that one of the pack-mules was missing, and not one of the men remembered seeing it after leaving camp this morning. The pack contained my shot-gun and case, with several blankets and valises. Three of the best men were sent back over the trail to try and find the missing mule, but at this hour (9 P.M.) the men have not returned, and I doubt very much if he is ever found.

Ambulances came in to-night from Ellis, bringing our mail. I received letters from home of July 20th, and a telegram of late date, saying all well and business running smoothly. We also got Chicago papers of July 28th and 29th, giving accounts of the failure of Duncan, Sherman & Co.

This day, August 10th, being my birthday, a grand dinner was given by Forsyth in honor of the event, and my health was drank most heartily, in champagne, claret, and ginger ale, and we sat at the table late. Songs were sung and stories told, and I shall not soon forget my thirty-fifth birthday in the Yellowstone Park.

Just after dinner the herder came in and informed me that there was a covey of dusky grouse near camp, whereupon I took my Winchester rifle, and on reaching the spot found the birds, an old hen and her brood, the chickens being full grown. There were twelve birds in the covey, and I fired thirteen shots, killing them all, and eleven out of the twelve were shot through the head. Baronette thought the shooting rather extraordinary, but I do not consider it so, as the birds were within thirty-five or forty yards of me and very tame, standing quietly, with heads erect, until the last one was killed.

August 11.—Mounting our horses at 6 o'clock this morning we rode over to Cinnabar Mountain, where the ambulances were waiting to take us on to Ellis. Doane accompanied the party, to see us started all right. We then bade him adiós, got into the ambulances, and were finally off at 8 o'clock.

We reached Bottler's at 1 P.M. and stopped for lunch. Found a fresh relay of horses waiting for us, and were off for Ellis at 2 o'clock. Just before leaving the Valley of the Yellowstone and about twelve miles from Bottler's, met Colonel Ludlow, of the Engineers, going in. His party was armed to the teeth, and had ammunition sufficient for an Indian campaign. They will, however, find but little use for guns in the Park at this season of the year.

We were late in reaching Rock Cañon, and it became very dark before we were half the distance through, and did not reach Ellis until 9 o'clock.

We have traveled, since leaving Ellis, one hundred and

thirty miles by ambulance and two hundred and fifty miles on horseback—total, three hundred and eighty miles.

The pack-train, when it returns to Ellis, will have traveled three hundred and twenty-six miles, as follows:

From Fort Ellis to Soda Mountain	65	miles.
" Soda Mountain to Black-Tail Deer Creek	8	"
" Black-Tail Deer Creek to Tower Falls	18	"
" Tower Falls to Cascade Creek	18	"
" Cascade Creek to Mud Volcano	14	"
" Mud Volcano to Lower Geyser Basin	26	"
" Lower Basin to Upper Geyser Basin	8	"
" Upper Basin to East Fork of Madison	15	"
" East Fork of Madison to Mud Volcano	19	"
" Mud Volcano to Yellowstone Lake, and return	12	"
" Mud Volcano to Fort Ellis	123	"
Total for pack-train.	326	miles

The Game and Fish of the National Park.

In 1870, when Lieutenant Doane first entered the Yellowstone Basin, it was without doubt a country unsurpassed on this continent for big game. Large herds of elk, mountain sheep, the black and white-tail deer, and the grizzly, cinnamon, and black bears were numerous. The Yellowstone Valley was swarming with antelope, and the mountain lion was frequently killed. During the past five years the large game has been slaughtered here by professional hunters by thousands, and for their hides alone. When the snow falls and the fierce winter storms begin in November and December, the elk, deer, and sheep leave the summits of the snowy ranges and come in great bands to the foot-hills and valleys, where they are met and shot down shamefully by these merciless human vultures. An elk skin is worth from six to eight dollars, and it is said that when the snow is deep, and a herd gets confused, one hunter will frequently kill from twenty-five to fifty of these noble animals in a single day. Over four thousand were killed last winter by professional hunters in the Mammoth Springs Basin alone. Their carcasses and branching antlers can be seen on every hillside and in every valley. Mountain sheep and deer have been hunted and killed in the same manner for their hides. The terrible slaughter which has been going on since the fall of 1871 has thinned out the great bands of big game, until it is a rare thing now to see an elk, deer, or mountain sheep along the regular trail from Ellis to Yellowstone Lake. There is undoubtedly considerable game still left on the west side of the Yellowstone, which, in the summer months, seeks the highest mountain summits to escape the flies and mosquitoes; and on the eastern side of the Yellowstone, commencing at the Lake and following the gigantic mountains northward, large game is probably as plentiful to-day as it was on the western side when Doane first explored this country. But few years will elapse before every elk, mountain sheep, and deer will have been killed, or driven from the mountains and valleys of the National Park. Already the hunters are looking to the eastern shore of the Yellowstone, and without doubt this coming fall and winter immense numbers of elk will be shot in this region for the paltry sum paid for their hides. It is an outrage and a crying shame that this indiscriminate slaughter of the large game of our country should be permitted. The act of Congress setting aside the National Park expressly instructs the Secretary of the Interior to provide against the wanton destruction of the game and fish found within the limits of the Park, and against their capture or destruction for the purposes of merchandise or profit. No attempt has yet been made, however, to enforce the act in the Park, and unless some active measures are soon taken looking to the protection of the game there will be none left to protect.

The time is coming when the whole world will visit this marvelous region, and if the game could be preserved from pot-hunters, there would be rare hunting sport found in this Park, for years to come, for those who shoot in season and in a proper manner.

How is it that the Commissioner of the Park allows this unlawful killing? The hunters who are doing this cruel and outrageous work are well known. Jack Baronette can point out and name the men who glide up to bands of elk on snow-shoes and shoot them down when too poor and weak to run away, or when the snow lies on the ground to such great depth that they are unable to travel, and fall an easy prey to their pursuers. In the name of humanity let this kind of hunting be stopped.

Game-Birds.—There is but one game-bird found in the National Park, and of this we killed some sixty in all. It is known as the Tetrao Obscurus, or Dusky Grouse. Professor Elliott Coues, in his elaborate work, "The Birds of the North-west," gives a description of this bird.

Wild Fowl.—In the fall and spring Yellowstone Lake and the numerous small lakes and ponds which everywhere abound in the valley are covered with every known species of American wild fowl. I have referred once before to the different varieties which I saw myself. Doane says he has never seen any country which equals the Yellowstone Lake and its adjacent waters for swan, pelican, heron, geese, and ducks. They come in countless millions in May, June, and October, and thousands remain here through the summer months and hatch their young.

Trout.—There is probably no river in the world the equal of the Yellowstone for big trout. They are found everywhere in this stream, from its sources to near its confluence with the Missouri. For hundreds of miles from the great lake north its waters fairly teem with these enormous fish, and a more vigorous, active, gamey fish I never wish to hook.

Above the Upper Falls of the Yellowstone many of the trout are wormy, and the impression seems to prevail that all the trout above the Falls are diseased and worthless for food, but I am satisfied this is a mistake. Those that are healthy and strong, and free from worms, can be told the moment they are landed. They are round and plump, the skin clear and fresh and the spots very bright, while those fish which are affected seem thin and poor and the flesh appears blood-red, and when hooked make but little play. We examined many of the latter, and found them full of long white worms, woven across the interior of the body and coming often through to the skin. It is generally supposed that the unhealthy condition of the trout above the Falls mainly arises from the chemical properties of the water. Mineral springs flow from the mountains and hills which surround the Lake, and its waters must be strongly impregnated by them. Below the Falls no diseased trout have ever been found. The East Fork of the Madison, Cascade Creek, and Fire Hole River have no fish in them; at least, we were unable to catch or see any.

At this season of the year the trout in the Yellowstone River and in the smaller streams will not often rise to a fly. Possibly earlier or later in the season they might be caught by fly-fishing. But with a good-sized hook and a brilliant fly, a grasshopper for bait, and two buckshot for sinkers, attached just above the snell, a person can have glorious sport anywhere he may chance to touch the banks of the Yellowstone.

Baronette told me of a mountain lake, twelve miles to the east of his cabin, which is literally alive with trout, running from four to six pounds. From his description of it, I should imagine it surpassed all trout lakes of the world. It lies high up the slope of a great snow range, the water clear, deep, and cold as ice, and he thinks no white man but himself has ever cast a hook in it.

August 12.—Our party has been quiet to-day.

August 13.—General Marcy and myself went to the Gallatin Valley to-day, where we had very good sport for two or three hours; killed and bagged twenty-six willow-grouse, seven long-bill curlew, and a number of jack-rabbits, returning to the post in time for dinner. The willow-grouse is a new bird to me, and is called a prairie-chicken here, but is not the pinnated grouse, although it resembles it, but is a smaller bird; the plumage on the breast much lighter, tail coverts shorter, head smaller, and the young bird, one-third grown, is feathered to the toes. They are very abundant in the Gallatin Valley, and with a well-trained dog two good sportsmen could bag a great number in a day's shooting.

General Forsyth got a note from Captain Hossack this evening saying the missing mule had been found and that the contents of the pack was all right. The mule was found, as we supposed, in a deep cañon near Tower Falls.

Soon after leaving camp at Baronette's and after crossing the main Yellowstone, the animal, in some unaccountable manner, slipped away from the packer in charge, and took the back trail to Tower Falls, and straying from the trail tumbled down the cañon. Baronette and two of the Cavalrymen found him forty-eight hours after he was missed lying upon his back in a deep gorge, with the pack partly off, and its contents but little injured. They took out the pack but were forced to leave the mule. Captain Hossack will take charge of my gun and other articles belonging to the party, and carry them through to Chicago, by way of Virginia City and Ogden.

The Secretary received a dispatch from General Sheridan this evening, dated yesterday, saying Mrs. Belknap, Mrs. Forsyth, and Mrs. Strong, and all the children were well.

Our visit at Ellis has been charming. General and Mrs. Sweitzer and Captain and Mrs. Ball, as well as the other officers, have done everything in their power to make our stay pleasant, and none of our party can ever forget their kindness and courtesy, and we are all under great obligations to them.

Captain Ball, with his company, left some days since for Camp Lewis, in the Judith Basin, to guard our party through to Carroll. Expect to meet him the second day out from Helena. The Indians have been very active for some weeks past along the stage-route between Helena and Carroll, particularly in the Judith Basin, and it is not considered safe to travel without an escort.

August 14.—We left Ellis, in a shower, at 5:15 o'clock, and made the first sixty miles in eight hours.

Soon after dinner we came to the Crow Creek Divide. As we struck the summit, the Missouri Valley lay before us, and in the dim distance the Missouri River could be seen. Immediately after crossing the divide we encountered an eight-mile stretch of rocky road, such as we have not traveled over before in a stage-coach. The track was filled with bowlders, over which we had to drive at a walk, and found it very uncomfortable and tiresome. Fifteen miles from Helena we took supper, and Mr. Clark put in the last relay of three spans of superbly-matched grays, the leaders being his own private team.

A few miles out from Helena we were met by a large delegation of the most prominent citizens of that place, who in carriages escorted us to the city. The first person I saw as the stage stopped was one of my oldest and dearest friends— Theodore Slosson, whom I had not met for years. He has been in Montana a long time, and is manager of the Legal Tender Mine, situated some sixteen or eighteen miles from Helena. It was a great surprise to me meeting him, and I was delighted beyond expression at once more shaking by the hand one with whom my early boyhood was passed, and for whom I have always had the highest regard.

I copy from the "Helena Daily Herald" an account of the reception given to our party, and the speeches which were made from the balcony of the hotel soon after our arrival:

In response to the notice in Saturday's "Herald," signed by prominent gentlemen of both parties, a large number of citizens—many of them accompanied by ladies—proceeded out on the Bozeman road Saturday afternoon to escort the Secretary of War and party into town. The coach was intercepted at Hartsall's, at the crossing of the Prickly Pear, seven miles from Helena, where the guests were taken in charge. These consisted of Hon. W.W. Belknap, Secretary of War; Randolph B. Marcy, Colonel and Inspector General; James W. Forsyth, Major of 10th Cavalry; George L. Gillespie, Major of Engineers; N.B. Sweitzer, Major of 2d Cavalry, commanding Fort Ellis, and General W.E. Strong, of Chicago. The party were transferred to carriages, and conveyed rapidly to the city in advance of the splendid six-in-hand with which Mr. Clark, by relays, had speeded them one hundred and twenty miles since the early morning.

Behind the distinguished guests, in vehicles strung out a quarter of a mile, drove the citizen delegation. The procession reached town just at dusk, entering by Rodney Street, filing down Broadway to Main Street and up Main to the International Hotel, where quarters for the party had been previously engaged. Here, awaiting the arrival of the Secretary, were the Silver Cornet Band, and a concourse of people, numbering, perhaps, two thousand in all. After an appropriate air from the cornets, Major Maginnis, Delegate in Congress, accompanied by General Belknap, appeared upon the balcony of the hotel, and in a neat, off-hand speech introduced the Secretary to the enthusiastic throng. The Major substantially said:

"MR. SECRETARY: It gives me great pleasure to welcome you on the part of this people—a pleasure enhanced by the remembrance of favors received from you in Washington, and of the fact that I never preferred a request on their behalf that did not meet with proper consideration and kind response from the head of the War Department. Among all the rulers of the nation I found in you at least one sympathizer with the frontiers in regard to the all-absorbing question of Indian management. You were always willing, so far as you could, to grant all calls upon you for assistance made by the Army officers to your Department. We had in you a Western representative in the Cabinet with a thorough appreciation of the wants and interests of the frontiers, and a hearty desire to stretch forth the hand of help to those feeble communities upon the rim of civilization. We are glad that you have come to see our mountains and valleys, and to ascertain the value of our mineral and agricultural wealth as a factor in the resources of the Union; that you have with your own eyes beheld the wonders of that enchanted land on the Yellowstone, and the romantic beauties of the Queen of the Mountain Territories; that you have traveled far wide of the usual summer resorts to examine the military needs of this wedge of settlements between the advancing settlements of the East and West—this thin line of mining towns and farming settlements, at present a mere band upon the very hem of Miss Columbia's Centennial garments, yet furnishing the gold and silver for her helmet and shield. You have observed for yourself the exposed condition of our Eastern frontier, and the necessity of strengthening the defense. We are especially glad to welcome you as our guest, and knowing that you will be glad to rest after your journey, I conclude by saying that I am the bearer of a large number of invitations to you from citizens of Deer Lodge, anxious not only to show you their necessities, but to entertain, and show you that the west side of the Territory has mountains as grand, lakes as large and clear, valleys as fertile, and mines as rich as any you have visited, and to show you that to the first Cabinet officer who has honored Montana with a visit the people of the Territory, from centre to circumference, extend a hearty welcome."

As the Secretary stepped forward he was greeted with three rousing cheers, following which he spoke about as follows:

"I am heartily surprised and gratified, gentlemen, not only at the extent but at the cordiality of this unexpected demonstration of welcome on your part, and at the kind words in which I have been introduced to you. Indeed, it is true that I have always sympathized with the difficulties under which the pioneers of the West have labored in their efforts to subdue the wilderness and to carve new commonwealths out of the vast domain of our country, and have, so far as I could, endeavored to aid and assist them. As you are, perhaps, aware, I have been in company with General Marcy and other officers of the United States Army, and with a dear friend of the old Volunteer service, visiting the grand region of the Yellowstone, and we have been delighting ourselves with its unequaled scenery. The majestic alpine peaks that surround it; the clear crystal waters that wind through it, coursing through cañons of awful depth, and breaking over waterfalls of surpassing height and beauty; its glades of green turf, interspersed with groups of trees that give the landscape the appearance of a natural park; its vast beds of wild flowers; its great mountain lake; its myriads of hot springs and other curiosities, and its grand geysers, sending vast fountains of water sparkling into the sunshine, fairly entitle it to the expressive name of Wonderland. I have also closely observed the more material aspects of your Territory, its fertile valleys and great stretches of grazing land. With the value of its mines I have long been acquainted.

I assure you that I have paid particular attention to the exposed condition of the Eastern settlements which I have traversed, and I assure you that the posts shall be reinforced and more troops sent to your Territory. I may say that I more fully appreciate your needs than before I came. You need a railroad, you need your water communication improved, you need more troops; indeed, you need strengthening and sustaining in every way that the General Government can do it; and, since I have seen and estimated the great resources of your Territory, and how well worthy they are of development, I assure you that, as far as I may be able, I will endeavor to aid in that development.

And now, ladies and gentlemen, as you know that we have just been on a long journey, I am sure that you will

General W. B. Sweitzer

allow me to again thank you for this cordial welcome, and to bid you a grateful good night."

After the Secretary had finished his speech he withdrew to the parlors of the hotel, and a large number of the best citizens, irrespective of party, called and paid their respects to him.

We made the drive from Helena, one hundred and thirteen miles, in twelve hours' driving time, averaging over nine miles an hour, and changed horses seven times.

August 15.—We attended Divine service this morning, and dined this evening with General A.J. Smith, Surveyor General of Montana, after which General Smith with a pair of dashing bays drove Colonel Gillespie and myself to the Hot Springs, four miles from the city, and we enjoyed the drive exceedingly. General Belknap, who is stopping at the house of General Potts, Governor of Montana, finds a good many Iowa people here, and has had numerous calls to return. Helena contains now about three thousand people, has several handsome buildings, and quite a number of its citizens are wealthy. The city is built in a gulch similar to Virginia City, and has suffered fearfully from fires, the principal business street having been swept clean three times. We cannot get away to-morrow as we anticipated. The Indians have run off so many animals from the stage stations along the route that considerable difficulty has been experienced in replacing them. The owners of the line, however, promise to start us on the morning of the 17th.

August 16.—We passed the morning pleasantly at the First National Bank in examining Mr. Hauser's magnificent collection of gold and silver specimens which have been collected from various mines in the Territory, after which we were invited by Mr. Hauser and a number of other prominent citizens to go to the Hot Springs and engage in a shooting contest with rifles. We drove out about 11 o'clock, and were handsomely entertained before the shooting began. Sides were finally chosen, and each gentleman took three shots, off-hand, at a four-inch "bull's eye" at seventy-five yards. General Sweitzer came the nearest to the centre at this distance. Then sides were chosen again, and the same number of shots fired at a smaller target at forty-five yards. General Sweitzer by a superb shot knocked out the very centre of the "bull's eye," and was unanimously declared to be the champion rifle-shot of Montana. I astonished the Helena gentlemen with my shingle-sight, firing eight shots at a white patch an inch and a half square at forty yards, and striking it six times. The Helena gentlemen pride themselves on their skill with the rifle, but General Sweitzer carried away the honors of the day.

Returned to the city at 3 o'clock, and at 4 were entertained at the St. Louis Hotel with an elegant dinner given to the Secretary and party by Mr. Hauser. After the dinner we called upon several ladies; then took a pleasant drive down the valley, stopping for awhile at the race-track, and upon our return visited the placer mines, where we saw the Chinamen at work, and in the evening attended a reception given in honor of the Secretary's arrival by Colonel Viall.

From the "Helena Daily Herald" I copy an account of the banquet given at the St. Louis Hotel, written probably by the Editor, Mr. Fisk, who was present:

Entertainment to Secretary Belknap and Party.

The banquet spread at the St. Louis Hotel yesterday, in honor and entertainment of Secretary Belknap and party, was an elegant and elaborate affair. Nine courses of fish, game, flesh, and fowl were part of the spread to which thirty jovial and keenly-appetized souls gathered themselves, with genial Sam Hauser, as host, at the head. There was eating there in plenty, and wine-drinking in moderate measure, and joking and story-telling, and a "show-down" of the happier faculties of speech, such as perhaps we shall not have again until the honored Secretary comes again, and his good friends with him. Toasts were not wanting, and the President, his War Minister, and the several guests down the table were fittingly alluded to as the feast went cheerily along. General Belknap, invigorated and built up by his mountain trip and tour through Wonderland, was the picture of rugged physical health. His girth of shoulders seemed more expanded, and a still stronger prop to the erect, massive head, and abundant shock of auburn whiskers, sweeping down from his handsome, intelligent face, and covering his broad chest. His response to the toast: "The health of the President," as also to that of "Our distinguished guest, the Minister of War," were elegantly worded, and delivered in that happy style for which his impromptu speech-making is noted. We regret that opportunity is not given us to report him, at least to the extent of placing on record the flattering mention he made of Montana, and the pictorial description bestowed upon the wonders of the National Park. Marcy, Strong, Forsyth, and Gillespie were also called to their feet, and responded in felicitous speeches.

Brief, pertinent, and neatly-executed responses, as they were called on, came from Colonel Sanders, Judge Knowles, Mr. Hauser, Colonel Smith, Governor Potts, Shirley Ashby, Major Maginnis, Judge Chumasero, Colonel Viall, Judge Wade, and others; the banquet pleasantly terminating in songs, with "Auld Lang Syne" as the finish. The Secretary and party, in company with several citizens, supplemented their dinner with a ride about the city, and a few calls upon old residents, whose latch-strings are always out to visitors. In the evening a reception was held at the residence of Colonel Viall, on Rodney Street, to which some two hundred of our people, old and young, married and single, hastened to meet the Secretary and party, and pay their respects. The occasion was the pleasantest of the kind that ever transpired in Helena. Refreshments were served at a seasonable hour, and a little later the company, bidding farewell to the guests and good night to host and hostess, withdrew to their homes.

Thus it will be observed that the people of Helena gave the Secretary and his party a warm and generous welcome. Indeed, several of the most prominent gentlemen gave up all business and devoted their entire time to entertaining us, so that we will long remember with pleasure our visit to the Capital of Montana, and the kind hearts of its citizens. Those who were most prominent in entertaining us were Democrats, and many of them bitterly opposed to the Administration; yet notwithstanding this they threw aside their politics, extended their hands, and opened their hearts to us.

August 17.—The Helena gentlemen were at the hotel in force this morning at an early hour to see us off. Sixteen miles from Helena we reached the summit of the divide, where we had an excellent view of Helena and the valley; then descended the mountain through Ferry Cañon, and crossed the Missouri at a rope ferry, eighteen miles from Helena; soon after which we took a lighter coach with four horses, and put our baggage in a heavy two-horse lumber wagon. The change was soon made, and we entered White's Gulch, twenty-seven miles out, at noon, where we got our first change of horses. From thence we passed up White's Gulch some five miles to a little mining hamlet, where we dined, and saw considerable placer mining. Water was very scarce at this season, but the miners told me they were able to make from $12 to $15 per day when water was plenty. Two miles from the town we came to the longest and steepest hill I have ever seen. Nothing in the park could begin with it for length. General Marcy says he never saw its equal on a stage road. It must have been nearly two miles in length, with a rise from the Gulch of from eighteen hundred to two thousand feet. As it was all the six horses could do to haul up the empty coach we walked the entire distance, and I can tell you "it was a breather if it wasn't."

At 5 o'clock we arrived at Camp Baker, which is garrisoned by two companies of the 7th Infantry, with General Gilbert in command. We dined here with Major and Mrs. Freeman, who set before us an elegant repast of brook trout, dusky and willow grouse, besides numerous other delicacies. Major Freeman caught to-day in a few hours, and within a short distance of the post, two hundred trout that would run from a half pound to a pound and a half.

At 8:15 o'clock left Camp Baker for Brewer's Springs, distant eighteen miles, reaching the Springs at a quarter before 11 o'clock, and having made seventy miles during the day. The springs are sulphurous, and their hygienic properties are highly appreciated in this Territory. Saw great numbers of grouse along the road to-day, but no other game.

August 18.—At 6 this morning we left Brewer's Springs, and made the first change at Copperopolis, twenty miles out, over a hilly and rough road, very much cut up by heavy freight wagons, reaching forks of Mussel Shell at noon, where we found a detachment of the Seventh Infantry and a Gatling gun, under command of Captain Rawn. Remained here till 1 o'clock, then pushed on for Judith Gap, distant thirty-two miles. This run was over a broad, rolling prairie, bordered in the distance by low ranges of mountains. The road was good, and we made excellent time, crossing a number of small streams, and among them I remember the Daisy Dean, Haymaker, and Hopley's Hole, or the Dry Fork of the Judith.

Just before dark I discovered a wolf on the crest of a ridge taking a deliberate survey of our party as we rapidly approached, and I gave him a shot from the wagon, while sitting in my seat, and killed him instantly, the bullet cutting out both eyes. I paced the distance, and found it to be over four hundred yards.

At quarter past 8 we reached Little Trout Creek, where we found Captain Ball with his company, waiting to escort us through to Carroll, the most dangerous section for Indians in this country. The night was dark, but the road fine all the way to Camp Lewis, and we made the trip of twenty miles in two hours and forty-five minutes; one-half the escort acting as an advance-guard, and the other bringing up the rear, and keeping close to the coach. In this order we arrived at Lewis at 11 o'clock, having traveled one hundred and ten miles in eighteen hours.

Camp Lewis is a summer cantonment, occupied by two companies of the Seventh Infantry, and commanded by Captain George L. Browning, who gave us a fine game dinner, served at midnight, with venison, dusky and willow-grouse, and brook trout. This camp is in the very heart of a famous hunting region—the Judith Basin—which is surrounded by the Judith Mountains and adjoining ranges, as well as by the Big and Little Moccasin. This section is swarming with grizzlies, elk, mountain sheep, and black-tail deer, but it is not considered safe to hunt here without a strong party, as hostile Sioux are comstantly lurking around in great numbers. Not more than four weeks since, a war party of these Indians made a dash down the valley and killed three or four of the soldiers of Captain Browning's command, who were hunting and fishing in sight of the post; and within two weeks the Crows and Sioux had a desperate battle, twelve miles up the valley, wherein the Crows were badly handled, and Long Horse, one of their head chiefs, killed. Troops have been very active on the road all the way from the forks of the Mussel Shell to Carroll, for several weeks past, and General Gibbon has distributed the forces under his command at the most exposed points, so there is no doubt about our getting safely through to Carroll.

I met this evening Doctor Hatch, an Assistant Surgeon, whom I had seen before, and who accompanied me on an expedition in Arkansas, in 1865, before I retired from the Army.

Antelope in considerable numbers were seen along the stage-road to-day, but were so shy that it was impossible to get near enough for a shot.

We crossed a number of fine trout streams to-day, in one of which (Little Trout Creek) two of Captain Ball's men caught, in two hours, three hundred trout that would run from one to two and a half pounds.

Captain Browning is a fine officer and a most agreeable and hospitable gentleman, who has done everything in his power to make us comfortable. Among other acts of kindness, he gave me this evening, a very fine mountain lion skin, which I shall take home as a memento of our visit.

August 19.—As the party moved out from Camp Lewis this morning Dr. Hart and I struck off on horseback for the Judith Mountain, intending to hunt along its base, and come into the stage-road fifteen or eighteen miles from camp. Captain Ball furnished me with a large, fine-looking horse, but without exception the roughest-gaited animal I ever mounted, and his canter was especially distressing. Dr. Hart rode an Indian pony, with saddle and accoutrements all of Indian manufacture; and when he came out of his tent prepared to mount, he was dressed in full Indian costume, and looked so much more like an Indian Chief than an Assistant Surgeon in the Army, that I told him if he had a few feathers in his hat he would readily pass for a Sioux brave about to take the war-path. I must confess I was not particularly anxious to leave the party and strike off alone into a country supposed to be swarming with hostile Sioux, but the Doctor assured me we would be in sight of the coach and escort most of the time, and that there was but little danger so long as we did not go too near the mountains.

Soon after leaving camp we saw great flocks of sage-hens, two of which I shot with my rifle, just to see what they were like, and found them a most beautiful game-bird. Those I killed were full-grown cocks, nearly the size of a hen turkey, probably weighing from six to seven pounds and at least two and a half feet in length, and in general appearance somewhat resembling the English pheasant. As these were the first sage-chickens killed on the trip, and the first I had ever seen, I gave them to my orderly, who fastened them to the cantle of his saddle and we moved on. After this we saw immense bands of antelope, at which I shot a great number of times, but as they were from five hundred to a thousand yards distant, and generally running, I failed to kill or hit one.

When we had been out from camp one hour and a half the Doctor stampeded me in earnest by declaring that he saw several Indians peering over a bluff on our right, which, if I may be allowed to judge, caused us to make good time towards the escort. At this particular juncture antelope-hunting had no further charms for either of us. After sharp riding, and having made from fifteen to eighteen miles across the country, we struck the stage-road, and soon after reached the coach and column.

At 1 P.M. we were at Box Elder Creek, (so named, I take it, because there is no Box Elder there,) having accomplished thirty-eight miles of our journey, and found Lieutenant Jerome, with a detachment, ready to relieve Captain Ball, and escort the party over the Bad Lands to Carroll. We rested here an hour, then moved on towards Carroll, forty miles distant. At Crooked Creek, sixteen miles from Box Elder, we struck the Bad Lands, (Mauvais Terres,) which is a famous buffalo range.

About twenty miles from Carroll saw the first buffalo, and from thence we continued to see them in small herds on both sides of the stage-road, but so far away that we did not pursue them. At length, however, we discovered a herd two or three miles in advance of us, and nearer the road, when Lieutenant Jerome and his orderly moved out of the column, crossed a deep ravine, and made straight for them. As soon as the coach came to a commanding point, nearly opposite the buffalo, which were quietly grazing, we halted to watch the chase; and soon we saw Jerome with his orderly dash swiftly down on the herd from the crest of a ridge that had, until this time, concealed them. In an instant the herd started rapidly to the south and directly away from the stage-road. It was a sharp and exciting race, but Jerome's horse soon carried him into the very centre of the flying herd. The dust raised in clouds, and for a short time hid hunter and game from sight; but as the buffalo reached the higher ground we could see them more distinctly, but they were then much scattered, showing that Jerome had pushed them hard; indeed, we could see a single horseman riding close beside a single buffalo, and the reports of his revolver, which we heard in quick succession, showed that the poor brute was doomed, and soon afterwards we discovered Jerome and his orderly slowly returning. They informed us on their return that they had killed one buffalo, and

W. E. Strong

could have killed more had they chosen to follow further.

About 5 o'clock a herd was discovered on the north side of the road, a mile or more to the front, working its way very leisurely down the hillside directly towards our road, where-upon the advance-guard halted till the coach came up, and the entire party exclaimed, "Now is your opportunity for a buffalo hunt." I did not need much urging, although I was a trifle nervous at first, as it was a new kind of hunting to me; yet nothing, I am sure, could have kept me back.

My First Buffalo Chase.

Lieutenant Jerome dismounted and gave me his horse, which was a fine animal, full of spirit, easy-gaited, and accus-tomed to running buffalo. Notwithstanding the fact of his having just made a long chase, the Lieutenant said the horse could carry me as fast and far as I would wish to ride. The Secretary of War loaned me his revolver, but could only find in the hurry and excitement of preparation twelve cartridges. Two Cavalrymen, armed with carbines and revolvers, and well mounted, were detailed to ride with me and be on hand to assist in case I was dismounted or met with any other mis-fortune. I moved cautiously to the front in advance of the escort, until I struck a deep ravine, crossing the stage-road, some six or eight hundred yards beyond which the buffalo were working their way slowly to the south towards larger herds, which we could plainly see grazing in the valley two or three miles distant.

Before coming out of the ravine I dismounted, tightened the saddle-girths, and saw that saddle and bridle were in perfect order, then placed six cartridges in my revolver and the remaining six in my vest pocket, in order to have them handy if wanted. The buffalo were at this time on the north side of the ravine, walking slowly along, stopping now and then to graze, but heading straight for the ravine and the road. I supposed the instant the herd discovered me it would wheel about and run directly back to the north. My plan, therefore, was to dash out from under cover of the ravine with all the speed my horse possessed, follow the south bank of it until the herd turned to the north, and then to cross at the first convenient point, following the herd whatever direction it might take. I was ready and nothing was to be gained by further delay, so grasping my revolver firmly in my right hand and telling the men to follow, I put spurs to my horse, and in an instant was fairly flying over the ground and rapidly approaching the game. My course lay along the southern bank of the ravine, which I saw at a glance would be utter folly for me to attempt to cross on horseback, in case the herd turned back. They did not notice me at first, but as I drew in rapidly on their front, cutting them squarely off from their course, they seemed suddenly to realize that they were being pursued. Much to my astonishment, however, they never turned from their course, but kept straight on towards the ravine.

When they first struck out I thought it would be an easy matter to head off the leader, and had singled him out as my prize when the race commenced; but I quickly found that I underestimated their speed and bottom, for I urged my horse at every bound, and he seemed to be doing his very best, and yet before four hundred yards were passed I saw that the leader and the two bulls nearest him were fairly outrunning my horse, and were likely to pass me long before I could get to close quarters. Not wishing to be beaten, I bore off more and more to the south, and at every jump of my gallant hunter sent home the rowels. As may be imagined the race at this time was more exciting than anything I had ever experienced. The blood fairly danced in my veins. No obstacle could have stopped me then I am sure, and I should have pushed my horse straight for any ravine, ditch, or stream that intervened between me and the running game. The country was rough and dangerous to ride over at such a pace. Sage-brush grew everywhere, heavy bowlders lay thick all around me, and several soft spots were encountered, wherein my horse sank to his fetlocks. Over and over again he stumbled, and twice he almost went down with me, but gathered himself quickly and right gallantly went on, losing but little ground. The race was at right angles, or nearly so, in the beginning, the herd running to the south and my course being nearly east, but gradually changed more to the south, as I saw the leaders were outrunning me. I paid not the slightest attention to the country I passed over, but kept my eye on the leader, while I urged my horse to his topmost speed.

When I finally struck the herd and came to close quarters, the leader and two others were at least one hundred yards in advance of me. Nevertheless I had beaten the remainder of the herd, so that they were on both sides and behind me; but the objective one was still in advance, keeping up spanking strides, when I crossed to the left through the herd, so as to have those in front of me on my right hand and then urged my horse again, in a straight-away race. How gallantly the noble animal responded to the spurs, carrying me across the

Carroll road, from whence I could see our party with the Cavalry escort at a commanding point in the distance, watching the chase. I ran away from the two Cavalrymen on the start, but looking back as I crossed the road I saw them drawing up on the rear of the herd. And now we raised a ridge running parallel to the road, and but two hundred and fifty yards to the south of it. There was a gradual descent here for a mile or more, and the ground was much firmer, affording my horse better footing and easier work than before; he was running his best, while great drops of white foam stood out upon his neck and shoulders, and his breathing was labored, but he never slackened his gait, and I could see now that we were gaining handsomely and drawing up on the nearest buffalo; and when I came alongside him he appeared to be suffering fearfully, and was blowing like a high-pressure engine, with mouth open and tongue out, and I could have touched him with my revolver as my horse shot by. The next one was reached and passed in the same manner, then another. And now I was alongside the leader of the herd, (a great, black, shaggy fellow, the strongest and fleetest of them all,) revolver in hand, cocked and finger on the trigger. I had won at last, although the poor brute had struggled manfully to leave me behind; but he had failed, and his pace was unmistakably becoming slower and slower, while his heavy breathing grew more sonorous and labored. Several times after getting to close quarters he dashed fiercely at me, but my horse was on the alert, and darting quickly to the left avoided him.

Up to this time I had not fired a shot. The run was so exhilarating, so intensely exciting, and so different from any

hunting I had ever taken part in, that I was in no haste to end
the sport. But as the time had now come for action, I brought
my horse so close to the great, shaggy monarch of the plains
that I could almost touch him with my pistol, and aiming
quickly back of his fore-shoulder, fired. The ball took effect,
but not in the right spot. Again and again I fired, but in each
case the bullet struck too high, the motion of my horse render-
ing it extremely difficult to take accurate aim. At the fifth
shot, however, he stopped and faced me, shook his head, and
made two or three desperate charges, but was so weak that I
easily avoided him. Great streams of blood flowed from his
mouth and nostrils, and he presented a frightful spectacle. As
soon as he became quiet I took most deliberate and accurate
aim, and with my sixth shot brought him down, and in a
moment more the leader of the herd lay at my feet dead.

For the first time I looked about to see where I was and
what had become of the remainder of the buffalo and the two
Cavalrymen, who, it appeared, had killed a buffalo off to my
right and rear, and were standing near it on their horses; and
the herd was scattered in every direction, but moving slowly
to the south, evidently well run down. Filling the chambers
of my revolver with the six extra cartridges, I singled out
another large bull near me, and, after a sharp and exciting
chase, brought him to bay and discharged all the cartridges in
my revolver without bringing him down, although he was
mortally wounded. Thereupon I called one of the Cavalrymen, and taking his Sharps' carbine, I dismounted, the man
holding my horse, and, as the bull at this time stood near the
bank of a small ravine which he was too weak to pass, I
crossed the ravine, so as to have it between me and the

wounded animal, as I knew it was considered dangerous to face one on foot; but I made up my mind he had not sufficient strength to get to me across the ravine, the banks of which were quite steep. He was not more than twenty-five feet distant, with his head close to the ground, and perfectly quiet. Taking careful aim I shot him in the curl above and between the eyes, and expected to see him drop dead in his track, but he merely shook his head as the bullet struck him, and I fired six shots as rapidly as I could load, hitting him each time in the same place, but the only response was a vigorous shake of the head at each shot. As I fired the sixth shot he turned around, took two or three steps to the rear, kneeled down, with his body resting against a bank, and was dead in another moment. It was the revolver-shots in his side that killed him, not those of the carbine in the head; for I examined, and found the six bullets had struck inside of a two and a half inch circle and were matted together against the skull, but did not penetrate or break it. The cartridge contained fifty grains of powder and the weight of the ball was three hundred and twelve grains, and yet the bullets failed to enter the buffalo's thick skull, although they were fired one after the other into nearly the same spot at a distance of twenty-five feet. Most extraordinary to my mind, and had I been told of such results I would not have believed them. I had no more shells for my revolver; the coach and escort had moved on; it was getting late, and as we were yet some distance from Carroll, I determined to give up the hunt, although with ammunition I could, without doubt, have killed several more that were still in sight; but I really had no desire to kill another, as it seemed cruel and wicked to shoot them down for mere pleasure. I took the tails of the two I had killed myself, and gave the carcasses of the three brought down by the party to teamsters of the Diamond "R" Line who came along about this time. After a sharp gallop of half an hour I overtook the coach, and gave up my horse, well satisfied with my first buffalo chase.

We reached Carroll at 9 o'clock, most thoroughly exhausted from the fatigue of our trip from Helena. The Secretary of War has been suffering terribly all day from a nervous headache, but is a trifle better this evening, and we earnestly hope he will be well in the morning. It is a severe journey we have made from Helena to Carroll, and in an open lumber-wagon (the usual vehicle), with the poor stock now on the road, it must be terrible. The Concord coach which brought our party was the first ever seen in Carroll.

The country passed over the last three days has not been particularly interesting. The day's ride from Helena to Brewer's Springs was, I think, the most agreeable. The Bad Lands, which we struck sixteen miles from Box Elder, must be very difficult to travel over in rainy weather. The road here is cut into great ruts by the heavy freight wagons of the Diamond "R" Line, and in many places there are from six to a dozen separate wagon tracks, showing that one road, if much used, soon becomes impassable.

Our mules had no water in crossing this section, as there was not a drop after leaving Box Elder until the Missouri was reached, nearly forty miles, and their sufferings were so great that they cried out continually during the last eight or ten miles of the trip.

In our thousand miles of stage-travel across Idaho and Montana we have had a large number of drivers, many of them strange characters; and as I have ridden the greater part of the journey on the outside of the coach, in order to have an unobstructed view of the country, I have had a good opportunity to study the characters of these peculiar specimens of the genus homo. The strangest and most interesting of them all was George Liscum, who handled the reins all the way from Helena to Carroll, and whose life and adventures would make a very readable book, as may be conjectured from the following incidents in his history:

George Liscum was born in 1835 at one of the posts of the Hudson Bay Company. His father, who at the time was a factor of that Company, is still living, and still holds the same position. Liscum is six feet in height, with a well developed physique, and his face slightly marked with small-pox. He was bound out to the Hudson Bay Company when a child, but ran away four times; was captured and carried back three times. Fought single-handed with a war party of Sioux at Judith Gap, killed six, wounded five and stampeded the rest. He was wounded in four places, and showed the scars. Killed in one night at Judith Gap, with poison, ninety gray wolves, and he declares it was not a very good night for wolves either. Lost nineteen thousand dollars on one horse-race and fifteen thousand at one hand of poker. In short, he was a gambler, miner, stage-driver, and Indian interpreter, speaking five different tongues. Served as a private soldier for a time in the Twelfth Illinois Infantry, and was at the battle of Donelson.

As we came upon the crest of the last hill overlooking Carroll, the Missouri River, for twenty-five miles in either direction, could be seen, and the moon coming out from the clouds full and bright at this instant added to the beauty of the scene. The lights from the little village below us glimmering through the tree-tops, and great bonfires were burning along the river's bank; and as the party reached Pinnacle Hill, a salute of seventeen guns was fired from a mountain howitzer, in honor of the Secretary's arrival. We dashed into Carroll at just 9 o'clock, amid the firing of guns and hearty cheers of the men. The "Josephine" not yet here, but expected by the 21st instant.

August 20.—The ride of yesterday morning on Captain Ball's rough-gaited horse and the run after the buffalo used me up completely. I am so stiff and lame to-day that I can scarcely walk, and must have taken a severe cold, as every bone in my body aches and my flesh is very sore.

A hospital tent has been erected on the bank of the Missouri, under the shade of large trees, and is occupied by the Secretary and General Forsyth. General Marcy has a good room in Mr. Clendenin's store, while Colonel Gillespie and myself occupy a mattress which, at night, is spread on the floor of the office of the Diamond "R" Company, so that we are all very comfortably quartered.

General Marcy has been hunting to-day with a Mr. Boyd, a hunter and guide of considerable renown in this part of Montana, and the General killed a black-tail deer (the only one seen), which Boyd packed in on his horse. Boyd said the General was sitting on his horse when he discovered the deer browsing in a thicket so dense that only the head and neck were in sight. Dismounting from his horse, he took careful aim and duplicated my shot in the Yellowstone Park, sending the bullet square through the deer's neck and killing it instantly. Boyd said the shot was a beautiful one. So the General and I are even now, each having killed a deer.

The rifle General Marcy has with him was made to order for him by Remington some two years since, and must be good, as the first four shots he made with it, near Fort Bridger, brought down three black-tail deer and an elk, and he killed with it at one time two deer and an elk in forty minutes. Upon this occasion the General had with him an orderly, who was a noted deer hunter, but not particularly demonstrative. When the General brought down the elk the man never spoke. Again the General fired, a few moments later, killing a deer handsomely. The hunter, however, uttered no word of commendation. But when the second deer fell before the General's deadly aim, he quietly remarked to the man that he thought this tolerable shooting, as it was all done in about forty minutes. The man could restrain his admiration no longer, but rushing up to the General, he exclaimed, "That's the best shooting I ever saw."

General Marcy is, without doubt, one of the most successful deer hunters in the country. He has had large experience and has studied the habits of the deer to such an extent that he knows just where to look for them, how to approach them, and when he shoots there is generally a dead deer. I was unable to hunt to-day on account of my crippled condition.

Carroll, which is a new town not shown on any of the maps, is two hundred and fifty miles below Fort Benton, a short distance below the mouth of Judith River, and nine hundred and ninety-one miles from Bismarck. It was established a year ago last spring by the Diamond "R" Freight and

Stage Line, represented by Mr. E. G. Maclay, Major Broad-water, and Mr. Carroll. This line carries freight, passengers, and the mail from Carroll to Helena, and to other points beyond in Montana. They run in connection with the Caulsen line of steamers, which connects at Bismarck with the Northern Pacific Railroad. The Caulsen line have this year the Government contracts for freight from Bismarck to Benton; have five steamers, viz: "Josephine," "Key West," "Far West," "Western," and "E. H. Durfy."

There are from thirty-five to forty houses in Carroll, and from seventy-five to eighty people; two billiard rooms, two hotels, two stores, a barber-shop, and numerous saloons, but "nary" a white woman in the town.

Mr. E. G. Maclay, the senior partner, who is stationed here during the summer months, is a most courteous and agreeable gentleman, and has done everything in his power to make us contented and comfortable.

This is the day fixed upon for the arrival of the "Josephine." General Forsyth had a dispatch at Helena, saying she left Bismarck on the 12th instant, and as she is the best, most reliable, and lightest-draught boat in the line, loaded with only one hundred tons of freight, and drawing but twenty-seven inches, Mr. Maclay thinks she will surely be here on time, or nearly so, unless some accident has befallen her. All we can do is to fold our hands and wait patiently, for the only way out of this country is by the Missouri River. We are about as effectually cut off from the world in Carroll as we were in the Great Geyser Basin of the National Park. There is a weekly mail to Helena, but the mail down the river is rather irregular.

135

This evening at 9 o'clock the steamer "C. W. Mead," of the Kountz Line (opposition), came in from above. She was crowded with passengers and very short of provisions. We might have taken passage on her, but as there was not a single state-room unoccupied, we decided to wait for the "Josephine." Twice to-day a man has been sent to Point Lookout, on Pinnacle Hill, to look for a boat, as from this point a steamer can be seen twenty-five miles below.

August 21.—No "Josephine" yet; she must certainly be here to-morrow, as this is her ninth day out from Bismarck, and unless she is fast on a bar or has met with some serious accident she must be very near. If anything has happened to her, we are in rather a precarious situation, as we cannot get back to Helena by stage there being no stock on the line that could take our party and baggage through. The escort has gone and the Government relays are beyond recall. We are trying to be patient, but this waiting day after day, with nothing to do, is wearisome indeed. We have read over and over again every book and paper we have, and about all there is to do is to sit in the shade, smoke and talk. General Forsyth's stories still hold out, but I am half inclined to think he is manufacturing the most of them. It does not matter much, as they are just as entertaining as those supposed to be true. The Secretary and Colonel Gillespie have told some good ones the last day or two, and General Marcy is able to entertain us with stories at any time. Marcy is anxious to hunt, but I am not able to ride and barely to walk. That morning hunt with Dr. Hart nearly killed me. There is a good billiard table here, and we have played considerable. Marcy, Forsyth, and Gillespie play a fine game.

We have found it very hot here every day from 10 to 2 o'clock, after which a fresh breeze springs up, and the remainder of the day is generally cool and delightful. Flies have annoyed us some, but there are no mosquitoes here.

August 22.—No "Josephine" yet, but she must be here to-morrow.

The Secretary this morning, in about five minutes' time, wrote some verses, which after showing me, he was about to destroy; but I prevailed upon him to allow me to read them to the party, and the decision was unanimous that they were too good to be lost and must go in as a part of the records for the trip. The following is a copy:

> *Waiting for the Steamer Josephine.*
>
> *My eyes are longing for the sight*
> *Of one I've never seen;*
> *I watch for her by day, by night—*
> *Beloved Josephine!*
>
> *They say her form is wondrous fair,*
> *Her movements full of grace;*
> *Her charms are so beyond compare*
> *I long to see her face.*
> *She walks the water like a bird*
> *Flying through woodlands green—*
> *Oh! where is he who has not heard*
> *Of my own Josephine.*
>
> *Thousands of miles I've traveled o'er,*
> *Fulfilling every duty,*

And longing each day more and more
  To gaze upon her beauty.
Oh! for a sight of the sweet charms
  Of her, my chosen queen,
I'd rest content within the arms
  Of darling Josephine.

Missouri's water slowly fall,
  Faster my fears arise,
As from the hills I look with all
  The strength of tearful eyes,
And watch for her for whom I wait
  With anguish sharp and keen,
Which only time can e'er abate,
  And lovely Josephine.

Oh! dearest, soon you'll surely come,
  Then vanish weary hours;
On her loved form she'll bear me home,
  And joy will then be ours.
But if she false and faithless prove
  I'll drink the gay benzine,
And drown forever all my love
  For heartless Josephine.

Carroll, Montana, August 22, 1875.

At 6 P.M. Mr. Maclay and I rode to the Pinnacle to take a look for the boat, and saw, a long distance down the river, what very much resembled the smoke from a steamer, which we watched through our glass for more than an hour, and at times we were quite positive the "Josephine" was coming, but

138

finally came to the conclusion that the smoke arose from a fire on the river bank. While on our way to Pinnacle Hill we saw a herd of sixty buffalo making its way from the bottom land to the high ground. They had been to the Missouri for water, and passed within half a mile of Carroll. I watched them through my glass for some time as they crept up the mountain in single file, and at length disappeared over the plateau at the summit. Night before last a large bull was shot not more than eighty rods from Mr. Maclay's office.

The day has hung heavily upon our hands, and we are beginning to get discouraged about the "Josephine," and fear she is fast on a bar or that some more serious accident has happened to her. If she does not put in an appearance to-morrow we shall begin to devise some plan for getting away from this place, and as there is a fine Mackinac boat here, owned by Mr. Clendenin, we may conclude to take that. General Marcy and I rather incline to this arrangement, as we can have splendid hunting for three or four hundred miles if we adopt this project, so that, upon reflection, we rather prefer the Mackinac to the "Josephine."

August 23.—The "Josephine" has not arrived, and we have about given her up. This is the fourth day we have been waiting and watching, and the conclusion we have reluctantly come to is, that some serious accident has happened to her. We are making preparations to man the Mackinac and go down the river in her to Bismarck, nine hundred and ninety-one miles. It is rather a dangerous trip, as we go through the very heart of the Indian country, where we are liable to be captured, but we have fully resolved to attempt it.

The boat is being overhauled and made as comfortable as

possible. It is thirty-eight feet keel, seven feet beam, two and a half feet hold, sharp at the bow and square at the stern, and has a tiller eight or nine feet in length; draws light, about three and a half inches; built to carry eight tons on a draught of fifteen inches; has four rowlocks placed forward of amidships. A rude cabin has been constructed in the centre of the boat, by putting up pieces of scantling seven feet long, supported on top by cross pieces and wagon covers thrown over and securely fastened, to keep off sun and rain. Two bunks have been made of rough boards, extending full length of cabin, and two and a half feet in width, and when covered with blankets and robes will make comfortable beds to lounge or sleep on. We have named the boat the "Diamond 'R,' " in honor of Mr. Maclay, who goes down as master of the craft. We have engaged Boyd for boatswain and pilot, with four oarsmen, one to do the cooking, so that we will have in our party eleven persons, each armed with a breech-loading rifle, with two hundred rounds of ammunition. We will wait till to-morrow afternoon, then, if the "Josephine" does not arrive, pull out with the "Diamond 'R.' "

George W. Boyd, who has general charge of fitting up our boat, is worthy of special mention. He is dreadfully deformed, having been born with club-feet and misshapen hands, but he is one of the most skillful guides and celebrated hunters on the Upper Missouri. He is thoroughly reliable in every respect, and his word as good, where he is known, as his bond. He has had great experience among the Indian tribes of this country, and can speak almost any of their dialects with fluency; besides, he is up to all their tricks; and as strange as it may seem, he can mount or dismount a horse quicker than I can, and is a capital rider. We all think very much of him, and congratulate ourselves in having secured so good a pilot for our boat.

Mr. Clendenin, a trader in Carroll, has been extremely kind and courteous to us, and we are under great obligations to him. Among other favors, he loaned us the Mackinac boat and several Winchester rifles for the party; besides, he presented me with a fine grizzly robe, and has given to each member of our party a choice skin of some kind.

August 24.—As the "Josephine" has not appeared, we spent the forenoon in getting our supplies and cooking utensils on board, consisting of twelve days' provisions for the party and a complete outfit for camping. A small mast has been put up forward of rowlocks, and a sail rigged for use whenever the wind is favorable. A pair of large elk horns and a buffalo head decorate the bow of our boat. At 2:30 P.M. we were embarked and ready to depart, with everybody in Carroll on the bank of the river to see us off. "Are you all ready, gentlemen?" says boatswain Boyd. "All ready," was the reply. Then, "Tie her loose," sings out the man at the helm. When the rope was cast off from shore the boat swung into the current, the men bent to the oars, and in an instant the "Diamond 'R' " was in motion, with her bow headed for Bismarck, distant only one thousand miles. Boyd's expression of "Tie her loose" was new to us. The Secretary remarked that if he should ever write a book he would adopt "Tie her loose" as his motto.

At 5:15 P.M. we had passed Ryan's wood-yard, sixteen miles from Carroll, having made eight miles an hour. One of our colored men, who hired to us as an expert oarsman, had unquestionably never before handled an oar. He made fearful work of rowing—catching crabs every other stroke; pulled his oar out of the rowlock; punched the man in front of him in the small of the back every time he raised the oar from the water. We tried for some time to teach him how to use the oars, but it was no use, and finally I relieved him, General Marcy taking the companion oar. Thus we pulled on for half an hour or more, when as we were turning a sharp bend in the river one of the men shouted, "There's a steamboat," and sure enough, half a mile below, was the bow of a steamer, her smoke-stack just coming into view around a bend. Some of the party thought it was the "Benton," others the "Josephine," but a few moments later we were near enough, with a glass, to read her name—"Josephine."

General Marcy and I were not particularly well pleased at the sight of the steamer, as we had become thoroughly tired of waiting and given her up altogether, accepting the Mackinac in her stead; and we had promised ourselves some rare sport in hunting between this and Fort Peck, two hundred and fifty miles below, as there is no part of Montana, excepting the Judith Basin, equal to this section of the Missouri for bears, buffalo, elk, and deer.

The "Josephine" soon came alongside, when we left the "Diamond 'R,' " and embarked with our baggage at 6 o'clock.

The "Josephine" left Bismarck on the afternoon of the 12th, and the Captain says he has used every effort to reach Carroll on time, but the low water and the transfer of his freight around several bars by yawl-boats has caused the delay. I do not think the Secretary and General Forsyth are altogether satisfied with this explanation, especially as the Caul-

"The Lovely Josephine"

sen line asked the privilege of sending a boat to Carroll to meet us, and agreed to have it at that point on the 20th. The boat should have had a light freight, and started from Bismarck early enough to have reached Carroll at the time agreed upon. Soon after we got on board the steamer laid up for the night, and the crew went ashore to collect wood. There being no wood-yards above Peck, each steamer has to cut its own fuel, which costs nothing but the labor.

We hope to reach Carroll early in the morning, so that the "Josephine" can discharge her freight and begin her return the following day.

Day before yesterday a party of men from Carroll manned an old Mackinac belonging to the Diamond "R" Company, and started down the river in search of the "Josephine," which they met one hundred and twenty-five miles below. They had fine success in hunting, killing several deer and elk, and are all on board the steamer returning to Carroll.

A few minutes after the Secretary stepped aboard the steamer from the "Diamond 'R'" he wrote some additional verses to the Carroll poem. They belong to the records, and I give them herewith:

> *She comes! She comes! I hear the sound*
> *Of her deep breathing, as around*
> > *The point her form is seen;*
> *With movement like Montana's fawn—*
> *Like the fleet deer upon the lawn—*
> > *Comes gliding Josephine.*
>
> *From the warm furnace of her heart*
> *Deep fires gleam out which make me start,*

And yet I love the scene,
As in the midst of darkest night
The air is brilliant with her light—
    The eyes of Josephine.

Moving upon the flowing tide
She gently presses to my side,
    And with her graceful mein
She seems like one sent from above,
To cheer me with her looks of love,
    And be my Josephine.

In the deep rapture of my soul
I give myself to her control,
    Calm, happy, and serene;
Clasped closely by her own fair hands,
Swiftly I sail to Eastern lands,
    Borne there by Josephine.

On Steamer "Josephine,"
Near Carroll, Montana, August 24, 1875.

August 25.—"Josephine" was in motion at daylight, and at 9 A.M. arrived at Carroll. As the boat was not to start back until the next morning, General Marcy and I resolved to have a deer hunt, and left Carroll immediately after in one of the "Josephine's" yawls, with five well-armed men and one day's provisions. We rowed down river as far as Lambert's wood-yard, twenty-five miles, where we are to-night occupying an unfinished log cabin. Our plan is to leave here at dawn in the morning, hunting some of the best points below until the steamer overtakes us. We are roughing it to-night on bread, bacon, and strong coffee, but as we anticipate good sport to-morrow morning we do not mind it.

August 26.—General Marcy and I spread our buffalo robes and blankets on the ground in one corner of Lambert's "oak-openings" cabin, and from my side next to the logs issued all sort of bugs and other insects, which amused themselves by crawling over my face and hands, and I do not remember ever being so nervous before. I rolled and tossed about all night, sleeping but little. Once I was startled by what I thought was an immense bonfire on a hill to the west. The light was streaming through the trees and through the open doorway of the cabin, and I roused General Marcy, who informed me it was nothing but the moon. I think the two or three cups of strong coffee which I drank just before retiring had something to do with my nervous condition. I was glad enough for an excuse to get up the moment the cook started a fire to boil our coffee, before daybreak. After taking a "hasty plate" of bacon and bread, we started off down the river at 4:30 A.M.

Our Morning Hunt.

The boat dropped quietly down the stream, the men pulling very gently at the oars, and two and a half miles from camp we came to an island in the river which we resolved to hunt, and landed from the boat at the upper end. The island was from two to three hundred yards in width and about three-quarters of a mile in length. General Marcy and Ingram selected the west side of the island, and Kennedy and I the east side. We hunted slowly and cautiously towards the lower end, marching abreast of each other like a skirmish line and keeping generally in sight. Fresh signs of elk and deer were abundant, and at nearly every step we expected to start game. The ground on my side, as I approached the lower end of the island, was difficult to hunt over on account of dense thickets of willows and rose-bushes which were higher than my head. I was within one hundred yards of the southern end of the island when I started a magnificent white-tail buck, that was lying in his bed within forty feet of me. He made one bound and wheeled about, facing me, with his tail flying high and head erect. I was so tangled in the rose-bushes, however, that to save my life I could not raise my arms and get my rifle into position to fire. I tried quietly at first to get loose from the dense thicket, and finally, by a desperate effort, succeeded in getting the gun to my face, but the buck was gone. One bound only into the copse, and he was out of sight. He ran directly towards the point where I supposed Marcy to be, and wishing to notify the General, I fired my rifle. In three seconds I heard a shot on my right, immediately followed by a second, and then a shout that the deer was killed. Making my way as fast as possible to the river, I found the General instructing the men in the boat to pull up opposite him, as the buck had disappeared under the water. It appeared that the General had fired at the buck while running, only getting a glimpse of him as he dashed through the dense covert towards the river bank, and plunged into the water, making directly for the main land. Marcy slipped in another cartridge, ran quickly to the bank, and killed the deer in the water at one hundred yards, shooting him back of the fore shoulder and through the heart. The deer struggled for an instant and sank, and it was half an hour before the men in the boat could find it. Finally, however, they discovered the antlers a foot or more under the water, and getting hold of them managed to tow the deer to the shore. It was a magnificent specimen, and would weigh nearly two hundred pounds. After properly dressing the animal it was loaded into the bow of the yawl, and we went on our way.

Two miles from the island we came to a point which Kennedy said was a good one for game, and we landed at the upper extremity, hunting in about the same order as before, Kennedy and I keeping furthest from the river. We had hardly reached shore when two white-tails bounded off from the bushes in our front and disappeared over a ridge. It was utterly useless firing, but I could not resist the temptation, and sent one shot after them. After going about half a mile without seeing any more game, Marcy and Ingram, who were on our right and a little in advance, started two black-tails, which sprang out of the bushes some distance ahead of us, but swung around in our direction, and passed within seventy-five or eighty yards of us, at full speed. I brought down one and Kennedy the other, very handsomely, both of which we packed to the boat, making three we had killed before 8 o'clock. Then we dropped down the river half a mile to another point, which we hunted in reverse order, myself and companion keeping close to the river and giving Marcy and Ingram the outside route. Kennedy started two large elk, but they kept in the thicket bordering the stream, so that although I heard them tearing through the brush, I was unable to see them. Two black-tail deer were started on this point, but they gained the foot of the bluffs, back from the river, before we saw them. As we approached the lower end of the point General Marcy discovered a large buffalo bull grazing in the open ground, three-quarters of a mile from us, and after getting to the leeward, Kennedy and I crept on him, under cover of a tree-top that had blown down, breaking partially off from the stump some seven or eight feet from the ground. Keeping this between us and the buffalo's head, and working constantly to the left, as he stepped along, we crept to the broken tree, which was within seventy yards of him. The old fellow, in the meantime, was grazing very quietly, wholly unconcerned and totally unconscious of our presence. Stopping a moment to catch our breath, we both fired together, taking deliberate aim. When the bullets struck him he must have made ten feet at the first jump and bore off to our right. I shot him three times with my Winchester while he was running fifty feet, and he then staggered and fell to the ground. General Marcy, who had stationed himself some hundred yards back, fired at the bull while running, hitting him in the body back of the shoulder, so that we all took part in the killing. I took the brush for my trophy, while Kennedy cut off a large piece of the "hump," and we went on to the lower end of the point, where the boat was awaiting us. Soon after which we heard the "Josephine" whistle, and when we got out of the willows found her waiting to take us on board, with our three deer and the buffalo meat, which we thought quite satisfactory for our brief morning hunt. Two or three hours more would undoubtedly have enabled us to kill eight or ten deer— possibly more—as the best hunting ground upon the river was a few miles below the point where the steamer picked us up, near the mouth of the Mussell Shell. However, it was perhaps just as well, for a severe storm of wind and rain came up soon after we embarked, and continued all day.

The "Josephine" left Carroll at 7 o'clock this morning and laid up for the night at 7:30, after making a run of one hundred and twenty miles.

We saw a number of deer this afternoon and a band of a dozen elk, which stood, just out of gunshot range, gazing at the boat as it ran by.

Our steamer has about forty tons of freight, and is drawing twenty-three inches, which causes her to strike now and then, but thus far she has gone over the bars with a jump, which makes her tremble all over. As yet we have had no serious detention, and expect to make Fort Peck sometime to-morrow afternoon, if good luck attends us.

The scenery along the river to-day has been quiet interesting. The banks of the stream, from six to ten feet in height, are generally thickly wooded, and covered with a dense undergrowth of cane, willows, and wild rose-bushes. All of the timbered points from Carroll to Peck abound with game.

Towards evening we came to the "Mauvais Terre" country, which is very broken and hilly, with elevated buttes of every imaginable form, and totally bare of vegetation, rising up in every direction. Ridges from one to five hundred feet in height also run at right angles with the general course of the river on both sides of it. Along the sharp crest of these high ridges, and clearly cut against the sky, could be seen forts and lines of breastworks; guns mounted in embrasures and en barbette; great mounds, shaped like castles, with turrets and drawbridges; churches, with spires to suit the fancy of all; round-top buttes, square, octagonal, and every other conceivable shape—many of them very beautiful. These formations are somewhat like those in the country west of Green River, but more curious and in greater variety.

Generals Belknap, Marcy, Forsyth, and myself had a game of whist this evening for the second time since leaving Chicago.

August 27.—The "Josephine" was in motion at daybreak, and made good progress till 9 o'clock, when she struck on a bar, and was sparred over a distance of six hundred feet, with only twelve to sixteen inches water. It is an interesting performance, this lifting and forcing a steamer bodily for hundreds of feet over sand-bars, where the water is much less in depth than the draft of the boat. One would hardly believe it could be accomplished without having seen it. We were six hours in getting over one bar, and our progress was at times so slow that considerable discussion arose among us as to whether the boat moved or not.

It has been a cold, rainy, disagreeable day, and we have been forced to remain in the cabin most of the time. About 4 this afternoon we saw a herd of fifty buffalo near the river, and a number of shots were fired at them, but they soon ran out of sight over a bluff.

We laid up at 8 o'clock within ten miles of Fort Peck.

Among the passengers on board are General Leisure and daughter, from Pittsburg, who are making the round trip from Bismarck. The young lady distinguished herself on the trip up the river by killing a wild goose with her father's rifle at two hundred yards from the pilothouse, and she shot twice at the buffalo this afternoon.

The steamer "Josephine," which was built in Pennsylvania in 1872 for Caulsen & Co. specially for the Upper Missouri trade, has made a good reputation as a fast and reliable boat. She is one hundred and eighty-three feet keel, thirty-one feet beam; measures three hundred tons, and draws light seventeen inches. She is named for General Stanley's daughter, whose portrait hangs over the door of the cabin. The boat has state-rooms for eighteen passengers aside from officers and crew, and is very comfortable. The party played "pedro" this evening till 9, and read from that time till midnight. Wind blowing a gale and raining hard.

August 28.—When we got up for breakfast at 6 o'clock this morning the steamer was taking on wood at Fort Peck, which was established in 1868 as an Indian trading-post by Messrs. Durfee and Peck. Subsequently it has been occupied as an Indian agency, and contains the agent's quarters, two or three warehouses, and a trader's store, all surrounded by a stockade.

In a defensive point of view I should consider the fort improperly located, as the buildings stand at the base of high bluffs, and in case of an attack from the east the occupants would be at the mercy of the attacking party, as the stockade would afford no protection. Several squaws were about the landing, and one of them came on board, taking a deliberate peep into every state-room en passant.

There are a number of Indian sepulchres near Peck, with the bodies wrapped in robes and suspended upon poles—the usual method of disposing of the dead among the Sioux. Many of them were seen at other points along the Upper Missouri.

Boyd, who left us here, presented me with a very handsome Indian gun-case made of buck-skin, heavily fringed with same material, and worked with beads.

At 11 A.M. we passed the mouth of Milk River, thirty miles from Peck, and an hour afterwards the boat was fast on a bar, which detained us until 1 o'clock.

In the afternoon the sun came out, and it was warm and pleasant the remainder of the day. The country becomes more and more level as we descend the river, the bed of which widens out, and in very low water great islands of sand appear almost everywhere in the river, and but little water in the main channel, which is extremely difficult to navigate. We ran along smoothly till 5:30, when we struck another bad place, which detained us an hour in sparring over. At 7:30 we reached Wolf Point, ninety miles from Peck, where the boat landed to let Ingram off, who goes through to Fort Buford by land.

At Wolf Point is one of the subagencies of Peck, and an Assiniboin Indian village is also located here. A reservation has been set aside for these Indians at this place, and the Government has furnished them animals and farming implements, and they appear to be making some progress as farmers. This is their first year, but they have good corn, wheat, and vegetables.

The arrival of a boat is a great event, and as the "Josephine" rounded a point two and a half miles up the river and came in sight we could see a great commotion in the village; and soon after they came rushing towards the river, so that by the time the boat arrived every Indian squaw and papoose was at the landing, presenting quite a novel and spirited scene, some on their ponies and others on foot—Indians, squaws, and papooses of all ages and sizes, and numerous Indian dogs. The young squaws and small boys seemed much more timid than the older ones. Wrapped in red blankets and half concealed in the thick underbrush which grew close to the river's bank, they peered at us with their sharp black eyes like so many wild animals. The tribe consists of fifty lodges, and each lodge averages about four, making two hundred all told.

We dropped down the river about ten miles from Wolf Point, and laid up for the night, where a supply of wood was cut and brought on board for to-morrow. We had our usual game of pedro this evening, fifty points up, which was won by General Marcy, after which we set for a couple of hours on the forward deck watching the boat's crew gathering wood and bringing it on board. Great iron jacks filled with pine knots were placed along the bank of the river, and the men carried torches, as the night was dark. It was an interesting scene, Negroes singing plantation songs and dancing as they returned from the boat to bring in a fresh load. We retired about midnight.

August 29.—Started at usual hour (daybreak), but were fast on a bar for about an hour. Soon afterwards struck Spread Eagle Bar about 6 o'clock, which is the same bar that Generals Sheridan and Forsyth, in the "Nick Wall," were fast upon for ten days in 1870, and after building dams and exhausting every known device to get off, were finally compelled to abandon the boat and go across the country to Buford. At 7:30 o'clock the "Key West" came in sight, bound up, with one hundred and forty tons of freight, and at 8 o'clock we were alongside of her.

Captain Coulson has decided that our freight must be transferred, and the "Josephine" return to Carroll, the "Key West" taking our party to Bismarck.

The "Josephine" is the only boat in the line that can, in low stages of water, navigate the river with any success from this point up. The "Key West" is a much larger and finer boat, having two hundred feet keel, thirty-four feet beam and four hundred and twenty tons burden, and draws light twenty inches. The delay is vexatious and annoying, but cannot be helped. We have been quiet to-day. Plenty of game all around us, but being Sunday did not hunt. This is the fourth day from Carroll, and we have only made three hundred and eighty-five miles. Our situation is anything but pleasant. When we left Ellis I expected to be home by the 26th or 27th, and to-day is the 29th, and we are still over six hundred miles from Bismarck. The delay is more annoying to the Secretary than any of us, I think, although he tries hard not to show it. We have read all the books and papers on board, and are driven to card-playing to kill time.

August 30.—The "Key West" left her landing at daybreak and made fair progress till 8 o'clock, when a strong wind arose which retarded the speed of our boat materially. The river is so narrow and the boat so large and light that she cannot be handled to advantage in such a wind as has been blowing to-day. We have, however, had but little difficulty with sand-bars to-day, and if the wind had been moderate, would have had a fine run. Laid up at dark fifty miles above Fort Buford, having made but one hundred miles. Country along the Missouri to-day generally level and uninteresting.

August 31.—Reached Fort Buford at 9:30 A.M. About two miles above the fort we passed the mouth of the Yellowstone, which is nearly as wide as the Missouri, with current very much swifter.

General Hazen, of 6th Infantry, and other officers of the regiment were at the landing to receive us, and the band played a number of airs very finely. We rode to General Hazen's (the commanding officer) headquarters in ambulances, where the officers of the garrison paid their respects to the Secretary and party. The troops turned out and marched in review before the Secretary and General Marcy, presenting a fine appearance, and with the best band we have heard on the trip. After the review we paid our respects to Mrs. Thibaut, Mrs. Bronson, and Mrs. Cowell, wives of the officers. General Hazen then showed us everything of interest about the post, after which we returned to the boat and were soon on our way again toward home. We enjoyed the visit at Buford exceedingly, as it was a pleasant change for us after five and a half days on the river.

Fort Buford was established in June, 1856, by Captain Rankin, of the 13th Infantry. Colonel Gilbert, of the 7th Infantry, was in command during the summer of 1870, but was relieved by General Hazen in the summer of 1872. From Buford to Bismarck, by water, is four hundred and fifty-nine miles, and by land two hundred and twenty-five; to Stevenson, by water, two hundred and seventy-five, and by land one hundred and fifty.

Buford is one of the best of the frontier posts. Everything about it is in the most perfect order. Warehouses, storehouses, barns, stables, and sheds admirably arranged and as neat as possible. The post has a bowling-alley, gymnasium, and billiard-room with three tables.

General Hazen's own house, where we were entertained, was a perfect little gem; walls frescoed after Eastlake and

155

covered with rare pictures; an upright piano in the parlor, and the rooms filled with beautiful things. The antlers of elk and deer and antelope hung in the halls, and some choice robes were scattered about, among which I noticed a white wolf-skin handsomely mounted. There was an air of comfort and elegance about the premises that one would hardly expect to find at a frontier post.

From Buford made eighty miles in the first six and a half hours' run, and a hundred and fifty miles during the day. If we have good luck we should be at Fort Stevenson to-morrow afternoon, and at Bismarck the day following.

September 1.—A dense fog hung over the river this morning, and the boat did not get under way till 8:30 o'clock. There seems to be a combination of the elements for the express purpose of retarding our progress. We cannot help but wonder what is in store for us. We are prepared for almost any calamity.

Passed some lovely country this forenoon—great broad plateaus, lying from fifteen to twenty feet above the bed of the river, and stretching away from one to three miles, ending abruptly in hills and buttes of most beautiful and varied form. Thousands of acres, smooth and level as a floor, coming down and touching the river, and covered with a rank growth of grass and flowers. Thousands of other acres of terraced lawns were seen, which were laid out with marvelous regularity, the rise of each terrace being from ten to twenty feet, and the face of each from fifty to seventy-five feet. I counted at one point five of these terraces, the highest one being at least a hundred feet above the grand plateau lying next to the river. The whole surface of the country is green with verdure. Every mile of river gained revealed something new and beautiful. Changes occurred in the general features of the landscape touching the river, and within sight, at every bend, and at almost every revolution of the steamer's wheel. I have been wrapt in wonder and amazement at the lovely panorama spread out for our inspection throughout the entire day. At 9 o'clock the sun came struggling through the clouds, and a little later the clouds disappeared, and although the wind has been high; the day has been charming.

We stopped to wood up at 12 o'clock, when Lieutenant Townsend and I went ashore, and put up two covies of sharp-tail grouse, ten of which I killed, but could only find six. The weather was very hot, and the mosquitoes so thick that they fairly drove us out of the woods.

September 2.—It commenced raining hard at daylight, accompanied by a strong wind, which soon increased to a furious gale, and was dead ahead. Nevertheless, at 10 we reached Berthold, where three tribes of Indians, the Mandans, Grosventres, and Arickarees, numbering about a thousand souls, are permanently located upon a reservation. They have been together on this reservation since about 1832, are very good farmers, and have excellent crops this year. General Otis told me they had four hundred acres of potatoes alone. The villages are on a high bluff, situated near together on eastern bank of the Missouri, overlooking it. The position is very commanding, and can be seen at a long distance, either ascending or descending the river. The lodges or tepees of the three tribes are similar in construction, frames made of cotton-wood and covered with earth.

A large number of the Indians came to the landing as the

boat touched, but they were a poor, ragged, miserable-looking set, and many of the older ones of both sexes half naked. We reached Fort Stevenson at noon, and found Lieutenant Colonel Huston and other officers of the post at the landing to receive and escort us to the barracks, about two miles distant. After spending an hour and a half inspecting the post we returned to the boat just in time to escape a storm of wind and rain so severe that the boat could not get away from the landing till nearly 4 P.M., so that we only made thirty-five miles before we were obliged to lay up for the night.

We were informed at Stevenson that General Terry has been at Bismarck waiting the arrival of the Secretary and party for more than a week.

Bismarck, September 3.—We arrived here at 10 A.M., and found General Terry, with two of his Staff officers, had been expecting us for ten days. General Mead, the General Superintendent of the Northern Pacific Railroad, had waited till the day before yesterday, when he returned to St. Paul. The Staff officers with General Terry are Major Barr, Judge Advocate, and Captain Hughes, Aide-de-Camp, who delivered to us upon our arrival quantities of letters and papers, most of them old, but a few of recent dates.

Our baggage was soon transferred to a car, and the "Key West" took us down to Fort Lincoln, where General George A. Custer, of the 7th Cavalry, commandant of the post, met us with several young officers, and drove us around the grounds, showing us everything of interest about the post.

General Custer directed the building of Fort Lincoln in 1873, and it is charmingly located and very attractive. The officers' and company quarters are most thoroughly built and their arrangement admirable. It has a magnificent parade ground, with the officers' quarters facing it on the west, and Custer's own quarters directly opposite the centre. The view one gets of the river and surrounding country from the elevated bluffs which rise up to the west of Lincoln is grand and beautiful.

General Custer is one of the most famous sportsmen in the country, and his outfit is more perfect than I have ever before seen. He has a large pack of magnificent English and Scotch stag hounds, and very frequently parties of ladies and gentlemen go out on horseback from the post to hunt antelope, which are abundant a few miles from Lincoln. Sometimes when the weather is fine these parties camp out, and spend two or three days running antelope and jack-rabbits with the full pack of hounds. Custer also has a shooting range, with regulation targets, most complete in all its arrangements and appointments, where he has done some fine shooting with his long-range Remington. He made one score of fifteen consecutive bulls' eyes, at five hundred yards, which I think has not been equaled. There is also a mile race-track near the post, and plenty of thorough-bred running and trotting horses. The General's house is handsomely furnished, and literally filled with the trophies of the chase brought down with his own hand. Upon the sofas and chairs in the parlors are spread robes of beaver and otter, beautifully mounted, and the floors are carpeted with the skins of bears, wolves, mountain-lions, and foxes. His library, just off the main hall as you enter the house, is filled with rare specimens of the big game of the West. The floor is covered with elegantly tanned and mounted robes of the grizzly bear, and suspended on the walls are the heads of grizzlies, buffalo, elk, deer, antelope, mountain-sheep, wolves, foxes, and other wild animals, mounted on shields. Indeed, I never saw such a collection, and the charm about it is the game was all killed by the General himself. In one corner of the room are suspended from the antlers of a deer a large and rare collection of Indian curiosities, which the General has gathered together in his numerous campaigns against the hostile tribes of the Western plains—implements of war and choice articles of Indian dress, pouches of every sort, medicine bags, and other things too numerous to mention. In another corner is a rack containing his target and hunting rifles, revolvers, hunting knives, shot-guns, and outfit for hunting complete. Books and rare photographs complete this gem of a room.

Mrs. General Custer showed great pride in this room containing her husband's trophies of the chase. She knew where every grizzly and buffalo was killed, and seemed to enjoy relating the particulars. We passed two delightful hours at General Custer's quarters. Mrs. Custer and Mrs. Calhoon, the General's sister, received the party most gracefully. The officers called and paid their respects to the Secretary of War; and we returned to the boat about 1 P.M., much delighted with our brief visit to Fort Lincoln, and reached Bismarck at 2 P.M., dined at the Capitol House, and left for home at 3 o'clock.

Bismarck contains about one thousand people, but I don't think any of our party were particularly delighted with the town or its people; on the contrary, we shook Bismarck dust from off our feet with genuine pleasure. Took supper at Jamestown, on James River, about half-past 10 at night, having traveled a hundred miles from Bismarck over a vast rolling prairie but little settled, although much of it is good grazing land. We spent the evening pleasantly in singing, and General Forsyth gave us some of his best Irish songs.

September 4.—Reached Fargo at half-past 6, where we got a good breakfast. This is a small village, but the houses, stores, and shops are well built. We here crossed the Red River of the North—Fargo on the west and a little station called Moorhead on the east bank. The Red River Valley is about forty miles in width, the two villages named being in about the centre of the valley, east and west. I have not, in all my travels, seen a more lovely stretch of prairie-land than this valley of the Red River. As far as the eye could reach, on both sides of railroad track, the country is level as a floor, and produces as fine wheat and other crops as one would wish to see. The soil black as ink, and very rich and deep. Not very thickly settled as yet, but wherever we saw a cultivated farm, the houses and other buildings were substantially and comfortably built, and would compare favorably with farm houses in Wisconsin and Illinois. Some day not far distant the whole of this Red River Valley must become a thickly settled and highly prosperous farming country. But little timber was seen except on the banks of Red River, where there is considerable.

Twenty-five miles from Fargo we came to a different section altogether. There is some fine prairie land, but it is dotted thickly with groves of timber. Oak openings were passed and numerous lakes were seen from one acre to twenty-five in extent, and many of them very pretty.

I have heard so much of the country along the Northern Pacific Railroad that I have taken great pains to see all I could of it from the cars. The station-houses along the road are excellent, and good taste is displayed in their construction. They are small, but the buildings neat and well built. At 1 P.M. arrived at Brainerd, where a good dinner awaited us. We saw the debris of the train that was wrecked at the bridge over the Mississippi, some time in July, I think. Two spans of bridge gave way, and the whole train was precipitated into the Mississippi, a distance of eighty feet, killing two persons and wounding several others. A new bridge has been built north of the old one, and it appears to be safe and strong. The engine of the wrecked train, which was badly damaged, has been elevated on timbers a few feet above the bed of the river preparatory to raising to the high ground. Brainerd is a small town, with two good-sized hotels or eating-houses, several stores, &c., and a number of fair-sized, well-built dwelling houses. The country for twenty-five or thirty miles east of Brainerd is very fair. After that thick timber skirts the road on both sides, with some small white and Norway pine and immense quantities of white birch, but we saw no timber of any great value. For the last eighty or hundred miles before reaching the junction, there is nothing but tamarack swamps and small lakes, utterly worthless for any purpose whatever that I can conceive of.

Reached Duluth at 6 P.M., where we had a good supper at the principal hotel. The ride to Duluth from the junction was perfectly charming, the road passing directly along the falls and rapids of the St. Louis River, which we had a good view of from the rear platform of our car, crossing a number of narrow gorges, but of great depth. The scenery is wild, picturesque, and beautiful, and would well compensate the tourist for a long journey. The waters of the St. Louis River for miles rush over a bed of rocky bowlders, and the descent is so great as to give a tremendous current, and form every instant cascades and rapids a little different from anything I have ever seen. The water is highly-colored, and the foam in the rapids and in the cascades is of a light creamy shade.

As to-morrow is Sunday we sang our last songs, and the evening passed most delightfully, and it was a late hour when the party retired.

St. Paul, September 5.—General Terry took us all to his own house for breakfast this morning, and we enjoyed beyond expression the fresh Spanish mackeral and other delicacies too numerous to mention which he set before us. We pronounced it the best breakfast by far that has been served on the trip, excepting only the one we ate at Kirby's, twenty miles out from Virginia City. General Terry's sisters, who keep house for him, received and entertained us most cordially, and we will long remember our agreeable visit at the General's house.

At 10 o'clock we bade General Terry and the members of his Staff good-bye, and left for Chicago. Nothing of interest occurred during to-day, but we sat up very late talking over the trials, tribulations, and pleasures of our long and most interesting journey, and finally retired about 2 o'clock.

Chicago, September 6.—Arrived at the depot at 6 o'clock. I said good-bye to members of the party before they were up, and in a few minutes more was at home.

We have been absent from Chicago fifty-three days, and Forsyth, Gillespie, and myself have traveled nearly five thousand miles, as the following will show:

Chicago to Omaha (rail)	500	miles.
Omaha to Ogden (rail)	1,025	"
Ogden to Salt Lake City and return (rail)	72	"
Ogden to Franklin (rail)	87	"
Franklin to Port Neuf Cañon (stage)	60	"
Port Neuf to Corbet's Station, on Snake River (stage)	60	"
Corbet's Station to Sand Holes (stage)	60	"
Sand Holes to Pleasant Valley (stage)	46	"
Pleasant Valley to Lovell's Station (stage)	70	"
Lovell's Station to Virginia City (stage)	70	"
Virginia City to Fort Ellis (stage)	85	"
Fort Ellis to Soda Mountain and return (ambulance)	130	"
Soda Mountain to Great Basin and Yellowstone Lake and return (horseback)	250	"
Fort Ellis to Helena (stage)	113	"
Helena to Carroll (stage)	258	"
On the Missouri (Diamond "R")	25	"
On the Missouri (yawl-boat)	50	"
Carroll to Bismarck (steamer)	991	"
Bismarck to St. Paul, via Duluth (rail)	602	"
St. Paul to Chicago (rail)	406	"
Total	4,960	miles.

RECAPITULATION

Traveled by rail	2,692	miles.
stage and ambulance	952	"
steamers	991	"
on horseback	250	"
Mackinac boat (Diamond "R")	25	"
"Josephine's" yawl	50	"
Total	4,960	miles.

Add to the above, for the Secretary of War and General Marcy, the distance from Washington to Chicago and return.

Our record of game and fish killed and taken is as follows

(strictly by our own party): Three buffalo, four black-tail deer, one white-tail deer, one wolf, sixty dusky grouse, seventy-five willow grouse, two sage-chickens, seven long-bill curlew, four jack-rabbits, and taken from the Yellowstone River, four hundred and eighty-nine trout, running from two and a half to four and a half pounds in weight.

Members of our escort killed, in addition to above, one grizzly bear, one buffalo, one antelope (Doane), and fifteen blue-winged teal, and, undoubtedly, caught, all told, three thousand large trout from the Yellowstone.

Purely as a hunting trip this was not a great success, for reasons herein stated, but as a fishing trip it has surpassed anything I have ever seen or ever again expect to see.